MW01001075

THE

LUXURY

COLLECTION®

GLOBAL EPICUREAN

3 Park Avenue, 27th Floor
New York, NY 10016, USA
Tel: 212-989-6769 Fax: 212-647-0005
www.assouline.com
ISBN: 9781614285922
Printed in China
Color separation by AltaImage
Art direction: Jihyun Kim
Design: Charlotte Sivrière
Editorial direction: Esther Kremer
Editor: Lindsey Tulloch

THE
LUXURY
COLLECTION®

GLOBAL EPICUREAN

ASSOULINE

CONTENTS

THROUGH A CHEF'S EYES

By Joshua David Stein

Chefs are made of the same basic material as the rest of us. They have the same senses; eyes of rods and cones; the same tangle of olfactory receptors behind their noses and carpet of taste buds in their mouths. Their fingertips are no more sensitive than normal, nor are the soles of their feet particularly more endurant.

But one need only stroll through a farmers' market to see that a chef lives in a parallel universe. Note how differently they peer at the stalls stocked with produce. We see a bin of kale or a pyramid of mangoes or the pearlescent scales of fish on ice. They, with a practiced evaluative gaze, make infinitesimal measurements of quality based on gradations of color and hue we might never have noticed. They can intuit freshness within a millisecond of seeing a leaf or stalk. A chef can pick up a mussel, and his or her muscle memory registers with precision whether it's "off" or not. (A lighter mussel suggests liquid loss.)

Chefs see what's in front of them, what came before them, and what is in the future. When local farmers deliver a whole lamb

Preparing the signature cheesecake at Hotel Bristol, Warsaw.

to Chef Alexandros Lefkaditis at Blue Palace in Elounda, a village on the island of Crete, for instance, he is reminded of the shepherd feasts that have taken place for centuries, in which the lamb is quartered and roasted over an open fire, eaten to the accompaniment of spontaneous poetry. He can see at once the past and, in the recipes he will prepare on the shores of the Sea of Crete, how that leads to the future.

To a newcomer, the cry of gibbons, the hoot of treetop barbets, the call of hornbills, and the tangle of vines and canopy of leaves seem like a chaotic and beautiful display. But to the chefs and naturalists of The Andaman in Langkawi, Malaysia, this is the best supermarket in the world. In the foliage, they find the small leaves of *kaduk* (*Piper sarmentosum*), an herb used to make *ulam*, a traditional Malay salad, as well as the small bright red peppers used in *sambal*.

Similarly, though the astonishing array of spices at Delhi's Khari Baoli, Asia's largest spice market, can be an overwhelming spectacle for an outsider, a chef like Manisha Bhasin of ITC Maurya navigates it deftly. A foodie might be able to guess correctly to identify some of the hundreds of brightly colored mounds of powder in silver bowls and fragrant seeds in burlap sacks, but a chef like Bhasin knows not just the spice but the spice monger too. She knows whose frankincense emerges from the tree pure white. She knows how many generations the masala masters go back, and the names of their fathers and sons. This treasury of knowledge, this way of seeing, is her life's work.

Across the world, at each of The Luxury Collection's more than one hundred properties, these instances of deep reading are repeated: Sussing out freshly made halloumi cheese and still-dewy mint at the markets in Broumana at Lebanon's Grand Hills; reading what Yucatecan soil will best receive the *cochinita pibil* at the Hacienda Puerta Campeche; plucking only the ripest apples from the choicest orchards in the heart of wine country at Las Alcobas in St. Helena. These acts, though not impossible for mortals, might be unnatural. But for chefs, they are simply a way to be.

Yet the true wonder of a chef isn't that she inhabits a richer world or sees ours differently. (Actuaries see our world much differently, too.) It's that she can share it with others, can somehow communicate these layers of history and tradition, the valence of culture and nature, and the relationships built through years of familiarity. A great chef isn't a sovereign. A great chef is an ambassador, an arbiter, and, ultimately, a companion too.

Rainforest dining at The Andaman, Langkawi, Malaysia.

THE
LUXURY
COLLECTION®
THE
LUXURY
COLLECTION®
THE
LUXURY
COLLECTION®
THE
LUXURY
COLLECTION®
THE
LUXURY
COLLECTION®
THE
LUXURY
COLLECTION®
THE
LUXURY
COLLECTION®
THE
LUXURY
COLLECTION®
THE
LUXURY
COLLECTION®
THE
LUXURY
COLLECTION®

STORY OF
THE LUXURY COLLECTION

The Luxury Collection is an ensemble of more than one hundred of the world's finest hotels and resorts, each noteworthy for its architecture, art, furniture, amenities, distinctive heritage, and cuisine. Our properties are bound together by a singular devotion to providing guests with authentic and unique experiences that are inextricably tied to each destination.

Within a world of hotels spanning myriad restaurants and bars over five continents, The Luxury Collection celebrates an incredible diversity of gastronomic culture. In this volume, *Global Epicurean*, we present a compendium of recipes and gourmet experiences, inspired and curated by The Luxury Collection's master chefs and mixologists.

Imagine yourself on a morning visit to Venice's storied Rialto Market to choose just-caught seafood and homegrown vegetables for an afternoon cooking class at The Gritti Epicurean School; being whisked around Seville to the city's most outstanding tapas eateries by Hotel Alfonso XIII's Andalusian guides; and honing your mixology skills at Palacio del Inka as you learn to make Peru's most authentic Pisco Sour. Discover why Ajman Saray's Golden Elixir epitomizes luxury in the United Arab Emirates; enjoy preparing your own version of fish and seafood, traditionally cooked in a *cataplana*, from Pine Cliffs Hotel in Algarve, Portugal; and delight in a dessert of Pebble-Shaped Rice Balls from The Grand Mansion in Nanjing that not only uses local ingredients but also celebrates the beautiful stones created by a natural river phenomenon in China. Each recipe and experience is a delectable homage to the surrounding environment and the ingredients it provides.

From the chili spices essential to Chef Konkangplu's Thai dishes in Bangkok to the fresh Venetian langoustines that find their way into Chef Turco's famous risotto to The US Grant's presidential spin on the classic Manhattan cocktail, each chef or mixologist's interpretation of his or her city's cuisine is bound to enchant and inspire. We hope you enjoy the diverse selection of flavors—and that they whet your appetite for culinary adventure.

AFRICA & THE MIDDLE EAST

The deck at Al Diwaan restaurant, Al Maha, Dubai

AJMAN SARAY

AJMAN, UNITED ARAB EMIRATES

THE GOLDEN ELIXIR

SERVES 1

For the honey saffron syrup:
1 Tbsp honey · 1 pinch saffron

For the Golden Elixir:
2 oz añejo tequila · 2 oz pineapple puree · 1½ oz Honey Saffron Syrup (above)
¼ oz freshly squeezed lime juice · Crushed ice, for topping off
Soda water, for topping off · Saffron, for garnish

1 Make the honey saffron syrup: Combine the honey and saffron with 2 Tbsp of water and whisk vigorously until well combined.

2 Make the cocktail: To a cocktail shaker, add the tequila, pineapple puree, honey saffron syrup, and lime juice. Shake well and strain into a golden pineapple tumbler. Top off with crushed ice and soda water. Garnish with a sprinkle of the saffron and serve.

“Honey is a luxury item in the United Arab Emirates and is produced locally. To combine it with saffron, which is considered the most expensive spice, makes this cocktail a luxury elixir.”

CHRISTOPHE THIBAULT
bartender, Ajman Saray

AL MAHA

DUBAI, UNITED ARAB EMIRATES

DATE SCONES

SERVES 10

$4\frac{1}{3}$ cups self-rising flour · $\frac{1}{3}$ cup granulated sugar · 2 Tbsp baking powder
$\frac{1}{2}$ tsp salt · 1 cup (2 sticks) plus 2 Tbsp unsalted butter, chopped and cold
$1\frac{1}{3}$ cups dates, pitted and chopped into $\frac{3}{8}$–$\frac{3}{4}$-inch pieces
1 cup plus 2 tsp heavy cream · 2 large eggs · Milk, for brushing
Clotted cream, for serving · Banana jam, for serving

1 Preheat the oven to 400°F. In a large bowl, sift together the flour, sugar, baking powder, and salt. Pinch in the butter with your fingers until the dough resembles breadcrumbs. Add the dates and combine, then create a well in the center of the mixture.

2 In a measuring cup, combine the cream and eggs and whisk until well combined. Pour the cream mixture into the well, then mix with a spatula just until combined.

3 Turn the dough out onto a clean work surface lightly dusted with flour and knead for about 45 seconds. Lightly wet your hands and separate the dough into twenty individual portions. Roll each into a ball and place on a baking sheet.

4 Brush the milk on top of each scone and bake for 10–15 minutes, or until the tops are golden. Serve with the clotted cream and banana jam.

Recipe by Piotr Kamieniczny, executive sous chef, Al Maha

AL MAHA

DUBAI, UNITED ARAB EMIRATES

PRIVATE DUNE DINING

Couples or groups of friends are invited to an intimate, secluded dining experience in the middle of the desert. This is magical fine dining under the Arabian sky at night—a picnic on a grand scale. The ambience, created by flame torches, Persian carpets, and starched white linen cushions, combines with the food to create a breathtaking memory. Field guides lead guests to a private spot where carpets, cushions, and a low-rise table are arranged for dinner. Guests will enjoy this private meal in the tranquility of the desert, complete with starter, main course, and drinks. Typically, guests are left to themselves; upon request, a waiter may remain for the duration of the meal. Once dinner is finished, the guide will return to gather diners at an agreed-upon time.

During this ultimate private dining experience, guests are surrounded by the tranquility of the dunes.

GRAND HILLS
BROUMANA, LEBANON

QUINOA TABBOULEH

SERVES 10

2 cups sunflower oil · 1 lb halloumi cheese, cubed · 3/4 cup all-purpose flour
1/3 cup black sesame seeds · 6 cups salted water · 3 cups red quinoa
2 2/3 cups diced fresh tomatoes · 1 cup diced onion · 2/3 cup olive oil
2/3 cup freshly squeezed lemon juice · 1/8 cup chopped fresh parsley
1/8 cup chopped fresh mint · 1/2 Tbsp salt · 1 tsp freshly ground black pepper
Romaine lettuce leaves, for garnish · Cherry tomatoes, for garnish

1. In a large, heavy pot with high sides over high heat, warm the sunflower oil. Coat the cheese cubes with the flour, then the sesame seeds. Drop the cheese cubes into the hot oil and fry for 2 minutes, or until golden. Transfer the cheese cubes to a paper towel–lined plate to drain.
2. In a large saucepan over medium-high heat, combine the water and quinoa and bring to a boil. Cook at a constant boil for 15–18 minutes, or until softened.
3. In a large serving bowl, combine the cooked quinoa with the tomatoes, onion, olive oil, lemon juice, parsley, and mint. Season with the salt and pepper and toss until thoroughly combined.
4. To serve, place the fried cheese cubes on top of the quinoa salad and garnish with the romaine lettuce and tomatoes.

GROSVENOR HOUSE
DUBAI, UNITED ARAB EMIRATES

MACADAMIA-CRUSTED HAMOUR, COCONUT–PUMPKIN SEED KHICHDI, BEETROOT KOKUM SAUCE, AND MANGO-PINEAPPLE SALSA

SERVES 4

For the ginger-garlic paste:
1 1/2 Tbsp peeled and chopped fresh ginger
2 cloves garlic, peeled and chopped

For the hamour:
2 Tbsp freshly squeezed lemon juice · 1 Tbsp Ginger-Garlic Paste (above)
8 (2 1/4 oz) boneless, skinless hamour or other whitefish fillets · 2 large eggs, beaten
1 tsp chopped fresh cilantro · 1 tsp peeled and chopped fresh ginger
1 tsp minced garlic · 1 tsp finely chopped green chili pepper · 1 pinch chili powder
5 1/4 oz macadamia nuts, shredded into flakes
1/4 cup vegetable oil, for searing · Salt, to taste

For the beetroot kokum sauce:
3 1/2 Tbsp vegetable oil · 1 tsp mustard seed
1/4 cup chopped fresh curry leaves · 1 tsp peeled and chopped fresh ginger
1 tsp minced garlic · 1 tsp finely chopped green chili pepper
1 red onion, thinly sliced · 4 whole dried kokum fruits · 2 cups coconut milk
1 small bunch cilantro, chopped · 2/3 cup pureed cooked beets · Salt, to taste

For the coconut–pumpkin seed khichdi:
1/3 cup vegetable oil · 1 tsp mustard seed · 1/4 cup chopped fresh curry leaves
1 tsp peeled and chopped fresh ginger · 1 tsp minced garlic
1 tsp finely chopped green chili pepper · 3/4 cup freshly grated coconut
1 cup basmati rice · 3/8 cup coconut milk
1/4 cup plus 2 Tbsp pumpkin seeds, plus more for sprinkling
1/3 cup plain yogurt · 2 Tbsp unsalted butter, cubed · Salt, to taste

For the mango-pineapple salsa:
2 Tbsp olive oil · 2 Tbsp chopped red onion
1 Tbsp freshly squeezed lemon juice · 1 Tbsp chopped fresh cilantro
1 1/4 cups diced mango · 1 cup diced pineapple · Salt, to taste

continued on following page

continued from previous page

1 Make the ginger-garlic paste: In a blender, combine the ginger, garlic, and 1 Tbsp of water and blend until smooth.

2 Prepare the hamour: In a wide, shallow bowl, combine the lemon juice and ginger-garlic paste. Add the hamour fillets to the bowl and season with salt. Marinate in the refrigerator for 30 minutes.

3 Preheat the oven to 350°F.

4 In a separate wide, shallow bowl, combine the eggs, cilantro, ginger, garlic, chili pepper, and chili powder. In a separate wide, shallow bowl, place the macadamia flakes.

5 In a sauté pan over medium heat, warm the oil. Remove the fillets from the marinade and add them to the pan. Sear for 2 minutes, or until golden.

6 Dredge each seared fillet first in the egg mixture, then in the macadamia flakes. Transfer to an oven-safe skillet or baking dish and bake for 3–4 minutes. Remove from the oven.

7 Make the beetroot kokum sauce: In a sauté pan over medium heat, warm the oil. Add the mustard seed. Once the oil begins to spatter, add the curry leaves, ginger, garlic, and chili pepper and sauté for 1 minute. Add the red onion and sauté for 2 minutes, or until the onion is translucent. Add the kokum, coconut milk, and cilantro and simmer for 5 minutes, or until the mixture thickens. Add the beets and season with salt. Remove from the heat.

8 Make the khichdi: In a sauté pan over medium heat, warm the oil. Add the mustard seed. Once the oil begins to spatter, add the curry leaves, ginger, garlic, and chili pepper and sauté for 1 minute. Add the coconut and sauté for 1 more minute.

9 Add the rice to the pan with 2 cups of water. Lower the heat and cook for 12 minutes, or until the water is absorbed. Add the coconut milk and the ¼ cup plus 2 Tbsp of pumpkin seeds and cook for 4 minutes, or until the rice is cooked. Remove from the heat. Add the yogurt and butter, stir to combine, and season with salt.

10 Make the salsa: In a deep bowl, whisk together the oil, onion, lemon juice, and cilantro. Add the mango and pineapple and season with salt.

11 To serve, place the khichdi in the middle of a serving platter and pour the beetroot kokum sauce on one side. Arrange the hamour fillets on top of the khichdi, along with the salsa. Sprinkle a few pumpkin seeds over the top and serve.

Recipe by Vineet Bhatia, chef patron, Indego by Vineet, Grosvenor House

VINEET BHATIA

executive chef, Grosvenor House, Dubai, United Arab Emirates

THE BEST SPOT FOR A COCKTAIL?

Geales, at Dubai Marina.

WHAT MAKES IT MEMORABLE?

A fantastic outdoor terrace with stunning views of the JBR (Jumeirah Beach Residence) skyline.

YOUR FAVORITE INGREDIENT TO USE IN COOKING?

Curry leaves.

IN WHICH RECIPES DOES IT WORK BEST?

Fish recipes.

WHAT IS A DISH NO ONE SHOULD VISIT THIS CITY WITHOUT EATING?

Lamb biryani.

YOUR PREFERRED TRAVEL DESTINATION FOR AN EPICUREAN EXPERIENCE?

Mauritius.

YOUR PREFERRED COMFORT FOOD?

Yellow dal and yogurt.

SHERATON ADDIS
ADDIS ABABA, ETHIOPIA

ABYSSINIAN

SERVES 1

$^{1}/_{2}$ fresh orange, peeled and seeded · 2 Tbsp finely chopped watermelon
2 Tbsp crushed ice · 1 tsp honey · $2^{2}/_{3}$ oz Ethiopian rosé wine, chilled
$^{1}/_{3}$ oz brewed Ethiopian coffee, chilled

1 In a blender, combine the orange, watermelon, ice, and honey. Puree until smooth.

2 Strain into a cocktail glass, top off with the rosé and the coffee, and serve.

“The Abyssinian cocktail is the height of luxury.”

MELAKU DESSIE
head barman, Sheraton Addis

SHERATON KUWAIT
KUWAIT CITY, KUWAIT

ROYAL HAMOUR FILLET, NAJDI RACK OF LAMB AND GULF PRAWN, SAFFRON MASH, BABY VEGETABLES, AND LEMON-BUTTER SAUCE

SERVES 4

1/3 cup plus 1 Tbsp olive oil · 1 small bunch fresh cilantro, roughly chopped
2 cloves garlic, peeled and minced · Ground cumin, to taste
3 oz rack of Najdi lamb (2–3 ribs), fat and trimmings removed
3 oz Persian Gulf royal hamour (brown spotted reef cod) fillet
4 large Spencer Gulf king prawns, washed, deveined, and patted dry
7 1/4 oz baby potatoes · 1/2 cup heavy cream · 2 Tbsp unsalted butter, divided
12 Iranian saffron threads · 1 head purple cauliflower, cut into florets
8 baby carrots · 4 ears baby sweet corn · Freshly squeezed juice of 1 lemon
2 violet or borage flowers, for garnish · 1 Tbsp red daikon cress, for garnish
Salt and freshly ground black pepper, to taste

1 In a large bowl, combine the oil, cilantro, garlic, and cumin. Place the lamb, hamour, and prawns in the bowl and marinate in the refrigerator for 12 hours.

2 Place the potatoes in a large pot and cover them with cold water by 1 inch. Place the pot over high heat and bring to a boil. Cook until the potatoes are fork tender.

3 Peel the potatoes and place them in a bowl with the cream, 1 Tbsp of the butter, and the saffron. Mash until smooth. Season with salt and pepper, cover with foil to keep warm, and set aside.

4 To a vacuum-seal bag, add the cauliflower, carrots, corn, and ½ Tbsp of the butter and season to taste with salt. Using a candy thermometer, bring a pot of water over low heat to 160°F. Add the sealed bag of vegetables to the pot and cook for 25 minutes. Remove the bag from the water and set aside.

5 Heat a charcoal grill to very hot, about 650°F. Remove the lamb and hamour from the marinade (reserve the marinade) and season them with salt and pepper. Grill until cooked through. Remove from the grill and cover with foil to keep warm.

6 Transfer the reserved marinade to a saucepan over medium heat. Cook until reduced and the texture is creamy. Add the lemon juice and the remaining ½ Tbsp of the butter and stir to combine. Adjust the seasoning as necessary. Remove from the heat.

7 To serve, arrange the lamb, hamour, prawns, mashed potatoes, and vegetables on a serving platter. Garnish with the edible flowers and red daikon cress and serve with rice and with the reduced marinade on the side.

ASIA

Cafe Hassui, Suiran, Kyoto

THE ANDAMAN
LANGKAWI, MALAYSIA

KASTURI ROYAL

SERVES 1

For the Pandan tea:
2 stalks lemongrass · 2 Tbsp peeled and sliced fresh ginger
2 pandan (a tropical plant) leaves

For the Kasturi Royal:
2 calamansi limes, sliced into wedges, divided · 3/8 cup Pandan Tea (above)
3/8 cup tamarind juice · 1 tsp raw sugar · 1 oz vodka · 1 Tbsp triple sec
Champagne, for topping off

1 Make the pandan tea: In a small saucepan, combine the lemongrass, ginger, and 5/8 cup of water and muddle well. Add the pandan leaves and bring to a boil. Remove from the heat and refrigerate until cold.

2 Make the cocktail: In a cocktail shaker, combine all but one of the lime wedges, pandan tea, tamarind juice, and sugar and muddle well. Add the vodka, triple sec, and some ice and shake well.

3 Pour over a strainer into a cocktail glass and top off with the champagne. Garnish with the remaining lime wedge and serve.

“The Kasturi Royal does not only define the vast array of local flavors of Malaysia but also showcases how indigenous ingredients can be used to concoct a flavorful and refreshing cocktail that is absolute bliss in a tropical setting.”

RAZIF SABRI
beverage manager, The Andaman

RAINFOREST MASTER CHEF

The experience begins with an educational walk in the lush, majestic ten-million-year-old rainforest surrounding The Andaman. Guided by the resort's naturalists, guests will identify the rainforest's herbs, such as *pegaga* and *kaduk* (wild pepper) leaves, and discover that not only can they be used to add distinctive flavors to food, but they are also believed to contain great medicinal properties. Guests will be immersed in the wildlife, watching macaques, dusky leaf monkeys, and flying lemurs in their natural habitat and observing how the forest's resources become their daily meal. Next, the resort's culinary experts offer a specially curated cooking class, educating guests on how Langkawi's indigenous herbs can be incorporated into various local dishes. The team-building challenge begins when guests are divided into groups to recreate a recipe using the knowledge they have gathered throughout the day.

From the forest to the kitchen table, guests are guided through a curated cooking class.

THE ASTOR HOTEL
TIANJIN, CHINA

INNOCENT'S DREAM

SERVES 1

2 oz vanilla ice cream · 1 oz single-malt Scotch whiskey
1 oz whole milk · 1/2 oz Monin vanilla syrup
10 ice cubes · 1/4 cup cacao powder

1 In a blender, combine the ice cream, Scotch, milk, vanilla syrup, and ice cubes and blend for 8–10 seconds.

2 Double-strain into a chilled martini glass, garnish with the cacao powder, and serve.

Recipe by Leo Li, chief bartender, The Astor Hotel

THE AZURE QIANTANG

HANGZHOU, CHINA

HAIRY CRAB MARINATED IN OSMANTHUS

SERVES 10

1/2 cup granulated sugar · 20 goji berries · 2 Tbsp salt
2 Tbsp olive oil · 3 Tbsp freshly grated ginger · 1 1/2 Tbsp chopped scallion
10 pieces (7 1/4 oz) whole hairy crab, thoroughly washed under cold running water
1 cup plus 1 Tbsp Chinese rice wine · 1 oz osmanthus flowers · 5 bay leaves
12 dried organic flowers · 2 limes, sliced

1. In a pot over medium-high heat, bring the sugar, goji berries, salt, and 5 cups of water to a boil.
2. In a wok over medium heat, warm the oil. Add the ginger and scallion and fry for 2–3 minutes. Add the fried ginger and scallion to the boiling pot and cook for 10 minutes to infuse the flavors.
3. Add the hairy crab to the pot and simmer for 12 minutes. Set aside to cool to room temperature.
4. Transfer the contents of the pot to a large lidded container. Add the wine, osmanthus flowers, and bay leaves and refrigerate for 6–8 hours.
5. Just before serving, top off the container with crushed ice. Transfer into bowls, discard the bay leaves, and garnish with the organic flowers. Serve with the slices of lime on the side.

Recipe by Veron Li, executive chef, The Azure Qiantang

THE CASTLE HOTEL
DALIAN, CHINA

ASSORTED SEAFOOD MENZI

SERVES 4

1/4 cup Chinese sesame paste · 1 1/2 Tbsp white vinegar · 1 Tbsp soy sauce
1/2 Tbsp chicken bouillon powder · 8 cups vegetable oil
14 1/2 oz Dalian menzi (a protein-rich starch paste), cut into 3/8-inch cubes
1 Dalian sea cucumber, sliced · 3 3/4 oz shrimp, peeled, deveined, and sliced
3 3/4 oz fresh squid, sliced

1. In a small bowl, whisk together the sesame paste, vinegar, soy sauce, and chicken bouillon powder. Set aside.
2. In a large, heavy pot with high sides over high heat, warm the oil. Drop the menzi cubes in the hot oil and fry for 1 minute, or until golden. Transfer the cubes to a paper towel–lined plate to drain.
3. In a large pot over high heat, bring 8 cups of water to a boil. Add the sea cucumber, shrimp, and squid and boil for 1 minute; remove the seafood from the pot and immediately plunge into a bowl of ice water.
4. In a large serving bowl, combine the menzi, sea cucumber, shrimp, and squid. Pour the sesame paste mixture over the top and serve.

“I still remember the menzi counter across the street: It was my dream every day to go there after school and have a spoonful of assorted menzi with garlic sauce. No other snacks can compare to that taste.”

BENSON LI
executive chef, Zhenbao Chinese Restaurant, The Castle Hotel

THE GRAND MANSION
NANJING, CHINA

YUHUA PEBBLE-SHAPED GLUTINOUS RICE BALLS

SERVES 4

2 cups glutinous rice flour · 1/3 cup granulated sugar
6 Tbsp wheat starch (found in Asian groceries) · 3/8 cup boiling water
5 Tbsp pork fat · 2 Tbsp unsweetened cocoa powder
Warm water, as needed · 6 oz red bean paste

1 In a large bowl, combine the rice flour, sugar, and wheat starch. Add the boiling water, then the pork fat. Stir until thoroughly combined and a dough forms. Separate the dough into three balls.

2 Press out one of the dough balls and add the cocoa powder and a little of the warm water to it. Knead until the dough becomes an even brown color. Divide the brown dough in half and roll the pieces into two cherry-size balls. Knead each ball into a long, thin cylinder.

3 Roll the two remaining dough balls into long, thin cylinders.

4 Press the two brown cylinders of dough into the white cylinders of dough, rolling them into a single long, thick strip of dough that is considerably longer than the original strips. Roll one-fourth of the resulting strip of dough into a ball and press it into a disk until it is about ⅙ inch thick; this disk will be used to make skins for the rice balls.

5 Place a spoonful of the red bean paste on top of the disk. Trim the edge of the disk to form a clean circle around the paste, then wrap the skin around it. Repeat three times to make a total of four rice balls.

6 Bring a large pot of water to a boil over medium heat. Drop the rice balls in the water and cook for 8–10 minutes, or until the balls float to the surface.

7 Transfer the rice balls to small bowls and serve.

“*Yuhua*, or rain flower pebbles, are a special decoration stone from Nanjing, polished smooth by the Yangtze River. To represent their different colorful textures, cocoa powder may be replaced with other ingredients, such as matcha.”

RONGBIN WEI
commis 1, The Grand Mansion

THE HONGTA HOTEL
SHANGHAI, CHINA

SHANGHAI-STYLE BRAISED STREAKY PORK IN SOY SAUCE

SERVES 4

14½ oz streaky pork, cut into a square · 1 Tbsp canola oil
1 cup plus 1 Tbsp huangjiu (a Chinese alcoholic beverage made from grains)
3 Tbsp soy sauce · 3½ Tbsp rock sugar · ½ tsp freshly grated ginger
½ tsp chopped scallion, plus more for garnish
1 dash dark soy sauce · Bok choy, steamed, for serving

1. In a large pot over medium-low heat, bring 6 cups of water to a boil. Add the pork and blanch for 1 minute; remove the pork from the pot and immediately plunge it into a bowl of ice water.
2. In a large, deep frying pan over medium-low heat, warm the oil. Add the pork to the pan and fry on each side for 15 seconds.
3. Add the huangjiu, soy sauce, rock sugar, ginger, scallion, and dark soy sauce to the pan and cook for 40 minutes, or until the sugar has melted. Reduce the heat to low and cook for another 40 minutes, or until the pork is tender and golden red.
4. To serve, place the pork in the center of a plate and surround it with the bok choy. Garnish the pork with the remaining scallion and serve.

ITC GARDENIA
BENGALURU, INDIA

KANE RAVA FRY

SERVES 4

1/2 Tbsp minced garlic · 1/2 Tbsp ground ginger
8 (1 lb) kane (ladyfish or skipjack) fillets, scored and heads removed
1 Tbsp plus 1 tsp lemon juice · 1 Tbsp plus 1 tsp chili powder
2 tsp ground coriander · 1 tsp ground cumin
2 cups plus 2 Tbsp sunflower oil · 1 3/4 cups semolina flour
10 fried curry leaves, for garnish · Salt, to taste

1 In a small bowl, combine the garlic and ginger to form a paste.

2 Place the kane fillets in a shallow dish with the garlic-ginger paste and lemon juice. Season with salt, then refrigerate for 30 minutes to marinate. Remove the fillets from the marinade and pat dry.

3 In a separate small bowl, combine the chili powder, coriander, and cumin. Apply the mixture liberally to the fillets and set aside for 15 minutes.

4 In a deep frying pan over medium heat, warm the oil. Coat each fillet with the semolina flour and place in the hot oil. Fry for 2 minutes, or until crisp. Remove from the pan and transfer to a paper towel–lined plate to drain.

5 To serve, transfer the fried fillets to a platter and garnish with the fried curry leaves.

ITC GRAND BHARAT
GURGAON, INDIA

BAJRA RISOTTO WITH CRISP OKRA

SERVES 4

$3^1/_2$ oz bajra (pearl millet) · 2 Tbsp ghee (clarified butter)
$1^3/_4$ tsp cumin seed · $^5/_8$ cup finely chopped red onion
2 tsp freshly grated ginger · 3 cloves garlic, peeled and pounded
$2^1/_8$ cups whole milk · $^1/_3$ cup freshly grated Parmesan cheese · 1 Tbsp light cream
$^1/_2$ tsp salt, plus more to taste · 1 cup slivered fresh okra
1 Tbsp plus $1^3/_4$ tsp chaat masala (spice mix)
1 Tbsp plus $^3/_4$ tsp red chili powder · $1^3/_4$ tsp ground coriander
$1^3/_4$ tsp ground turmeric · $^1/_4$ cup besan (chickpea flour) · $1^3/_4$ cups olive oil

1. Soak the pearl millet in 6 cups of cold water for at least 3 hours, or overnight. Drain.
2. In a heavy, lidded saucepan over medium heat, warm the ghee. Add the cumin seed and cook for a few seconds, or until it crackles. Add the onion, ginger, and garlic and sauté for 5–7 minutes, or until golden. Add the milk and pearl millet and simmer for 30–45 minutes, or until the millet is soft and fully cooked. Season with salt, then add the Parmesan and cream. Reduce the heat to low and cook for 1 minute. Stir until thickened to form a risotto. Remove from the heat and cover to keep warm.
3. In a mixing bowl, combine the chaat masala, chili powder, coriander, turmeric, and the ½ tsp of salt. Dredge the okra in the mixture. Transfer the okra to a separate bowl and sprinkle with the chickpea flour.
4. In a frying pan over medium-high heat, warm the oil. Add the okra and fry for 1–2 minutes, or until crisp. Transfer to a paper towel–lined plate to drain.
5. To serve, ladle the risotto onto a serving platter and place the crisp okra on top.

Recipe by Shivneet Pohoja, executive chef, ITC Grand Bharat

ITC GRAND CENTRAL
MUMBAI, INDIA

MUMBAI CUTTING CHAI

SERVES 1

For the Assam tea:
2 tsp granulated sugar · 1/2 tsp freshly grated ginger
1 pinch ground cardamom · 2 Tbsp Assam tea powder · 1/2 cup whole milk

For the Mumbai Cutting Chai:
1/4 cup blended Scotch whiskey · 1/8 cup Assam Tea (above)

1 Make the Assam tea: In a small saucepan over medium heat, heat the sugar and ½ cup of water. Add the ginger, cardamom, and tea powder. Simmer gently over medium heat for 5–6 minutes. Stir in the milk and set aside to cool.

2 Make the cocktail: Combine the whiskey and tea in a tea kettle with ice. Strain into a cutting chai glass and serve.

ITC GRAND CHOLA
CHENNAI, INDIA

TAMARIND MARY

SERVES 1

For the simple syrup:
¼ cup granulated sugar

For the Tamarind Mary:
3 oz tamarind juice · 2 oz vodka · 2 Tbsp freshly squeezed lemon juice
1½ Tbsp Simple Syrup (above) · 2 dashes Tabasco · Lemon wedge, for garnish

1 Make the simple syrup: In a small saucepan over medium heat, combine the sugar with ¼ cup of water. Cook for 5–7 minutes, stirring until the sugar has dissolved. Set aside to cool to room temperature.

2 Make the cocktail: In a cocktail shaker filled with ice, combine all the ingredients except the lemon wedge.

3 Shake and strain into a sugar-rimmed Old Fashioned glass. Garnish with the lemon wedge and serve.

“This cocktail features well-integrated notes of the famous Byadgi chili from Karnataka, as well as tangy homemade tamarind syrup. Best enjoyed with an Indian meal.”

SHAARIQ AKHTAR
food and beverage manager, ITC Grand Chola

ITC KAKATIYA
HYDERABAD, INDIA

MUTTON SHIKHAMPUR KEBAB

SERVES 4

For the chana dal (makes 2 oz):
1/2 cup chana dal (split Bengal gram, a lentil similar to chickpeas)

For the kebab:
1/4 cup plus 1 Tbsp roughly chopped garlic · 2 Tbsp freshly grated ginger
1 cup ghee (clarified butter) · 1 medium white or red onion, peeled and sliced
2 lb lamb, washed, boned, and patted dry · 2 oz Chana Dal (above)
1 tsp dried seeded chopped red chili pepper · 1 tsp salt
1/2 Tbsp black peppercorns · 1 1/2 tsp green cardamom · 1/2 tsp cloves
1/2 tsp ground black or royal cumin · 1 cinnamon stick · 1 bay leaf · 8–10 saffron threads
2 tsp chopped fresh cilantro · 1 tsp chopped fresh green chili pepper

For the stuffing:
1 medium onion, peeled and chopped · 3 1/2 Tbsp hung curd (yogurt drained of all its water)
2 Tbsp chopped fresh mint · 1 Tbsp chopped fresh cilantro
1 tsp chopped green chili pepper · 1 1/4 cups ghee (clarified butter), for cooking
Mint chutney, for serving

1 Prepare the chana dal: To a saucepan, add the chana dal and just enough water to cover it. Set aside to soak for 1 hour. Place the saucepan over high heat and bring to a boil. Cook for about 35 minutes, or until the chana dal is mushy. Remove from the heat and drain off any excess water.

2 Make the kebab: In a mortar and pestle or the bowl of a food processor fitted with the "S" blade, combine the garlic and ginger with 2½ cups of water and grind or process into a fine paste. Set aside.

3 In a large, heavy pot with high sides over high heat, warm the ghee. Place the onions in the hot ghee and fry for 8 minutes, or until browned. Transfer the onions to a paper towel–lined plate to drain. Reserve the ghee.

4 In a heavy copper pot over medium heat, combine the lamb and chana dal. Rub the ginger-garlic paste over the lamb and into the chana dal until evenly coated. Add the chili pepper and season with the salt and peppercorns.

5 In a piece of cheesecloth, combine the cardamom, cloves, cumin, cinnamon stick, bay leaf, and saffron. Tie securely, making a bouquet garni, and place the bouquet garni in the pot.

6 Add 1 quart of water and the reserved ghee to the pot. Bring to a boil and cook for 45 minutes, or until the lamb is tender. Skim and discard the fat from the surface of the liquid and continue braising for 20 minutes, or until semi-dry. Remove from the heat and discard the bouquet garni.

7 Transfer the contents of the pot to the bowl of a food processor fitted with the "S" blade and pulverize to a grainy texture. Refrigerate for 20 minutes.

8 Make the stuffing: In a small mixing bowl, combine the onion, curd, mint, cilantro, and chili pepper and mix gently.

9 Portion the pulverized meat into ¼-cup spheres and stuff them with the stuffing mixture. Press the spheres into galettes (flat disks).

10 In a large frying pan over medium heat, warm half of the ghee. Add the galettes and cook, while drizzling the remaining ghee over them, for 2 minutes on each side, or until they are browned, crisp, and evenly cooked.

11 Place on a serving platter and serve hot with the mint chutney.

ITC MARATHA
MUMBAI, INDIA

VADA PAV

SERVES 4

For the dry chutney:
1/8 cup grated coconut · 2 tsp chopped Byadgi chili pepper · 1 clove garlic, peeled · Salt, to taste

For the green chutney:
1/2 cup chopped fresh cilantro · Freshly squeezed lemon juice, to taste · Salt, to taste

For the red chutney:
1/4 cup tamarind pulp (medium-thin consistency; if thicker, thin it by adding water)
1 Tbsp plus 1 tsp jaggery (palm sugar)
1 tsp freshly ground black pepper · Salt, to taste

For the vada mix:
3 Tbsp vegetable oil · 6–7 curry leaves · 1/2 tsp ground turmeric
2 tsp finely chopped fresh green chili peppers · 1 tsp peeled and chopped fresh ginger
1 tsp chopped garlic · 1 tsp crushed coriander seed · 1 tsp mustard seed · 1 cup mashed potatoes
2 tsp chopped fresh cilantro · Salt and freshly ground black pepper, to taste

For the vada batter:
1/2 cup besan (chickpea flour) · 1/2 tsp ground turmeric
1 pinch baking soda · Salt, to taste · 2 cups vegetable oil

For serving:
4 pav (ready-made Indian bread rolls) or medium burger buns
4–5 fried green chili peppers

1 Make the dry chutney: In a dry pan over low heat, toast all the ingredients until fragrant. Let cool, then transfer to a mortar and pestle. Grind into a coarse powder and set aside.

2 Make the green chutney: In the bowl of a food processor fitted with the "S" blade, combine all the ingredients and process into a smooth paste. Set aside.

3 Make the red chutney: In the bowl of a food processor fitted with the "S" blade, combine all the ingredients and process into a smooth paste. Set aside.

4 Make the vada mix: In a sauté pan over medium heat, warm the oil. Add the curry leaves, turmeric, chili peppers, ginger, garlic, coriander seed, and mustard seed and sauté for 3–4 minutes. Remove from the heat. Add the potatoes and cilantro and mix well. Season with salt and pepper and mix well again to blend all the ingredients. Form the mixture into four small (2¾-oz) dumplings and set aside.

5 Make the vada batter: In a mixing bowl, combine the chickpea flour, turmeric, baking soda, salt, and ¼ cup of water. Mix into a thick batter; if needed, add a little more water. Set aside for 5 minutes and stir well before use.

6 In a deep frying pan over medium heat, warm the oil. Coat the vada dumplings evenly with the vada batter and deep-fry each until golden. Transfer the dumplings to a paper towel–lined plate to drain.

7 Slice the pav in half and spread each half with green chutney. Place a fried vada dumpling in each bottom half and replace the tops. Serve hot with the chutneys and fried chili peppers.

“The Vada Pav is truly the most iconic yet humble street food snack, capturing the vibrancy and character of Make in India in Mumbai.”

MAYANK KULSHRESHTHA
executive chef, ITC Maratha

ITC MAURYA
NEW DELHI, INDIA

AMARANTH AND WINTER PEA KEBAB WITH NARANGI ORANGE MURABBA AND TAMARIND CHUTNEY

SERVES 4

For the tamarind chutney:
1/2 cup jaggery (palm sugar) · 1/3 cup tamarind pulp · 1 tsp ground cumin
1 tsp freshly ground black pepper · 1 pinch red chili powder · Black salt, to taste

For the narangi orange murabba:
5–6 segments Indian orange · 2/3 cup granulated sugar · 7–8 cloves · 1 (2-inch) cinnamon stick

For the amaranth and winter pea kebabs:
1 oz amaranth seeds · 1/4 cup ghee (clarified butter), divided · 1 onion, chopped
1 green chili pepper, chopped · 1 lb red and green amaranth leaves, washed and chopped
3/4 cup fresh winter peas, pureed · 1/3 cup besan (chickpea flour), toasted
2 tsp peeled and chopped ginger · 1 tsp garam masala
4 (4-inch) bamboo or wooden skewers, soaked in water
2 tsp chopped fresh cilantro, for garnish · Salt, to taste

1 Make the chutney: In a heavy pan over low heat, combine all the ingredients with 1 cup of water and cook for 30 minutes, or until the mixture thickens. Set aside.

2 Make the murabba: Separate the orange segments and remove the seeds. In a heavy pan over low heat, combine the sugar, cloves, and cinnamon stick and fold in the orange segments. Cook for 15 minutes, or until softened.

3 Make the kebabs: In a dry skillet over low heat, toast the amaranth seeds for 3–4 minutes, or until lightly browned.

4 In a skillet over medium-high heat, warm half of the ghee. Add the onion and green chili pepper and sauté for 2–3 minutes, or until the onion is translucent. Add the amaranth leaves and cook for 7–8 minutes, or until wilted. Add the peas and cook for 10 minutes, or until the moisture evaporates. Fold in the chickpea flour to bind the mixture and cook for 8–10 minutes, or until thickened. Fold in half of the toasted amaranth seed, the ginger, and the garam masala, and season with salt.

5 Shape the contents of the skillet into 3 disks and coat each disk with the remaining amaranth seed. Place an equal number of the disks on each of the prepared skewers.

6 In a skillet over medium heat, warm the remaining ghee. Place the kebabs in the skillet and cook on each side for 3–4 minutes, or until golden. Remove from the heat.

7 To serve, place an equal amount of the tamarind chutney on four serving plates and place a kebab on top of each. Garnish with the cilantro and orange murabba and serve.

Recipe by Manisha Bhasin, senior executive chef, ITC Maurya

ITC MAURYA
NEW DELHI, INDIA

FOOD SHERPA AT KHARI BAOLI
ASIA'S LARGEST SPICE MARKET

A mind-boggling variety of sinfully rich dishes, tangy spices, and myriad historical flavors have been brought to New Delhi by the various settlers who have made the capital their home. The chef, acting as a food Sherpa, helps guests uncover the culinary tapestry of Delhi found in the city's colorful bylanes and bustling marketplaces. Passionately guiding guests around New Delhi's most popular gastronomic destinations, the food Sherpa relates fascinating legacies and behind-the-scenes secrets and provides insider tips on which foods travelers cannot miss while visiting.

“Food Sherpa is a great initiative by ITC hotels, as it showcases unique local street cuisine which may not otherwise be experienced. As an initiative to revive the past and our commitment to artisan foods and techniques, the event encourages local masters and presents their foods on ITC menus. I constantly scan the market for unique foods which later find their way onto our menu.”

MANISHA BHASIN
senior executive chef, ITC Maurya

Above: Chef Manisha Bhasin. *Opposite:* An abundant selection at Khari Baoli market.

200
400

ITC MUGHAL
AGRA, INDIA

ANAAR-E-KALEE
(POMEGRANATE BLOSSOM)

SERVES 1

2 oz freshly pressed pomegranate juice · $1^2/_3$ oz London dry gin
$^1/_2$ oz freshly squeezed lemon juice · $^1/_3$ oz simple syrup
2 pieces green cardamom, peeled · 1 pinch black salt · $^1/_2$ pinch ground cinnamon
1 pomegranate blossom, halved, for garnish · Pomegranate peel, for garnish

1 In a cocktail shaker filled with ice, combine the pomegranate juice, gin, lemon juice, simple syrup, cardamom, black salt, and cinnamon.

2 Shake well and strain into a chilled martini glass.

3 Garnish with the halved pomegranate blossom and peel on a long wooden pick and serve.

“Like a crown jewel, the Anaar-E-Kalee is a cocktail with an exotic combination of freshly pressed pomegranate pearls enhanced with subtle spices and the flavor of juniper berries, offering indigenous flavors of the royal Mughal era.”

GITENDAR
bartender, ITC Mughal

ITC RAJPUTANA
JAIPUR, INDIA

LAAL MAANS

SERVES 4

For the ginger paste (makes 1/3 cup):
1 1/4 oz fresh ginger, peeled · 3 tsp sunflower oil · 1/2 tsp salt

For the garlic paste (makes 1/3 cup):
15 cloves garlic, peeled · 3 tsp sunflower oil · 1/2 tsp salt

For the laal maans:
1 1/4 cups peanut or sunflower oil · 1 tsp whole garam masala · 1 1/2 lb onions, sliced
1/3 cup Ginger Paste (above) · 1/3 cup Garlic Paste (above)
1 1/8 lb lamb chops, washed and dried · 1 1/8 lb boneless leg of lamb, washed and dried
2 1/2 Tbsp Kashmiri red chili powder · 1 tsp ground coriander
1 tsp ground garam masala · 2 cups plain Greek yogurt, beaten
Fresh cilantro leaves, for garnish · Salt, to taste

1. Make the ginger paste: In a blender, combine the ginger, oil, and salt and blend until smooth.
2. Make the garlic paste: In a blender, combine the garlic, oil, and salt and blend until smooth.
3. Make the laal maans: In a large, heavy pan over medium heat, warm the oil. Add the whole garam masala and cook for 5 minutes, or until it crackles. Add the onions and sauté for 10 minutes, or until golden brown. Add the ginger and garlic pastes and cook for 2 minutes. Add the lamb chops and leg and cook for 10 minutes, or until browned. Add the chili powder, coriander, and ground garam masala. Season with salt and cook for 15 minutes. Add the yogurt and cook for 10 minutes. Season again with salt and cook for 20 minutes, or until the lamb becomes tender and the oil floats to the top. Garnish with the cilantro and serve.

CARLOS MOTA

interiors stylist

YOUR FAVORITE LOCAL PLACE TO EAT?

Peshawri at ITC Rajputana in Jaipur.

YOUR BEST MEAL THERE?

The lamb!

YOUR FAVORITE INGREDIENT IN A DISH?

Chili peppers, olive oil, and truffles.

WHAT IS YOUR FAVORITE FOOD AND DRINK PAIRING?

Red wine and chocolate.

THE BEST QUALITY ABOUT THE LOCAL CUISINE?

The use of local, organic ingredients.

YOUR PREFERRED TRAVEL DESTINATION FOR AN EPICUREAN EXPERIENCE?

Italy, Spain, and India.

YOUR PREFERRED COMFORT FOOD?

Roast chicken with potatoes and crispy bacon.

ITC SONAR

KOLKATA, INDIA

GONDHORAJ AND LEMONGRASS BRAMBLE

SERVES 1

For the lemongrass infusion:
6 stalks lemongrass, finely chopped · 2 cups granulated sugar

For the Gondhoraj and Lemongrass Bramble:
1 Gondhoraj lime peel · 1/3 cup Lemongrass Infusion (above)
2 oz Grey Goose vodka · Crushed ice, as needed
1 stalk lemongrass, for garnish

1 Make the lemongrass infusion: In a small saucepan over medium heat, combine the lemongrass and sugar with 2 cups of water. Stir together and simmer for 5 minutes. Strain, reserving the liquid.

2 Make the cocktail: In a collins glass, lightly muddle the lime peel. Add the lemongrass infusion and vodka. Add crushed ice until the glass is half full and stir with a swizzle stick. Top off with more crushed ice and stir gently. Garnish with the lemongrass stalk and serve.

Recipe by Soumen Dey, restaurant manager, Pan Asian, ITC Sonar

“Paying tribute to the social fabric of the destination, the Gondhoraj and Lemongrass Bramble brings together varied flavors, reflecting the amalgamation of several cultures in the city.”

GAURAV SONEJA
food and beverage manager, ITC Sonar

ITC WINDSOR
BENGALURU, INDIA

BANANA DOSA WITH CORIANDER AND COCONUT CHUTNEY

SERVES 5

For the coriander and coconut chutney:
2 cups freshly grated coconut · 1 cup roughly chopped fresh cilantro
¾ cup roughly chopped fresh mint · 2 whole green chili peppers
¼ cup freshly grated ginger · 1 Tbsp tamarind paste · 1 clove garlic, peeled
1 tsp salt · 1 Tbsp plus 1 tsp sunflower or soybean oil
1 tsp white urad dal (lentils), split, without skin · 2 whole red chili peppers
4 sprigs curry leaves · 1 tsp mustard seed

For the banana dosa:
3⅓ cups overripe bananas, peeled · ⅔ cup rice flour
¼ cup finely chopped cashews, fried · 1 Tbsp superfine sugar
⅓ cup ghee (clarified butter)

1 Make the chutney: In a blender, combine the coconut, cilantro, mint, green chili peppers, ginger, tamarind paste, garlic, and salt and blend until the mixture reaches a slightly coarse texture. Transfer to a lidded container.

2 In a frying pan over medium heat, warm the oil. Add the urad dal and sauté for 1 minute, or until the lentils are lightly browned. Add the red chili peppers, curry leaves, and mustard seed and cook for 30 seconds.

3 Add the urad dal mixture to the lidded container. Mix well and refrigerate until ready to serve.

4 Make the dosa: In a mixing bowl, mash the bananas into a rough paste. Add the flour, cashews, and sugar and whisk together.

5 In a nonstick frying pan over medium heat, warm the ghee. Spoon the banana mixture into the pan and cook on each side for 2½ minutes, or until golden.

6 Transfer the dosa to a serving platter and serve hot with the chilled chutney.

KERATON AT THE PLAZA
JAKARTA, INDONESIA

YELLOWFIN TUNA SAMBAL DABU-DABU

SERVES 4

For the sambal beberok:
$^{1}/_{8}$ cup chopped ripe tomato · $^{1}/_{8}$ cup chopped green tomato · $^{1}/_{8}$ cup chopped shallots
1 tsp chopped red chili pepper · 1 tsp freshly squeezed lime juice · 1 tsp coconut oil
$^{1}/_{2}$ tsp chopped bird's eye chili pepper · Salt, to taste

For the tuna:
2 Tbsp coconut oil · $1^{3}/_{4}$ lb sashimi-grade yellowfin tuna · Salt and freshly ground black pepper, to taste

For the dabu-dabu sauce:
$^{3}/_{4}$ cup seeded and finely diced tomato · 2 kaffir lime leaves, finely julienned
$^{1}/_{4}$ cup thinly sliced shallot · $^{1}/_{4}$ cup sliced red chili pepper
1 Tbsp freshly squeezed lime juice · 3 tsp coconut oil
Salt and freshly ground black pepper, to taste

For the baby corn and rice:
$^{2}/_{3}$ cup baby corn · 1 cup cooked glutinous rice · 2 Tbsp grated coconut
2 Tbsp Javanese brown sugar · Salt and freshly ground black pepper, to taste

For serving:
Chopped fresh cilantro, for garnish · Kecap manis (sweet soy sauce) · Peanut sauce

1. Make the sambal beberok: Combine all the ingredients in a mortar and pestle or the bowl of a food processor fitted with the "S" blade and grind or process into a paste. Set aside.
2. Prepare the tuna: In a large skillet over high heat, warm the oil. Season the tuna with salt and pepper and sear for about 1 minute on each side, or until the inside is medium rare. Set aside for about 2 minutes before slicing.
3. Make the dabu-dabu sauce: In a mixing bowl, combine the tomato, lime leaves, shallot, and chili pepper. Season with salt and pepper, drizzle in the lime juice and olive oil, and stir to combine.
4. Make the baby corn and rice: Season the baby corn salt and pepper. Warm a grill or griddle to very hot and grill the corn until well charred on both sides. Remove from the heat.
5. In a mixing bowl, stir together the rice, coconut, and brown sugar and stir until well combined.
6. To serve, slice the tuna thinly and place it on a platter with the grilled corn and dabu-dabu sauce. Place the rice beside the tuna, garnish with the cilantro, and serve with the kecap manis, peanut sauce, and sambal beberok.

Recipe by Donny Kumala, executive chef, Keraton at the Plaza

THE LAGUNA
NUSA DUA, INDONESIA

AYAM BETUTU
(ROASTED CHICKEN IN BANANA LEAVES)

SERVES 6

For the chicken:
1 (3 1/3-lb) whole chicken, rinsed and patted dry · Banana leaves, for wrapping

For the seasoning and stuffing:
18 shallots, peeled, halved, and sliced · 6 cloves garlic, peeled, halved, and finely sliced
3 stalks lemongrass, finely sliced · 5 fragrant lime leaves, finely sliced
1 (2-inch) piece fresh ginger, peeled and chopped
1 (3-inch) piece fresh turmeric, peeled and chopped
1 (3-inch) piece fresh kencur (aromatic ginger) root, peeled and chopped
6 candlenuts, chopped · 3 Tbsp coconut oil · 1 1/2 Tbsp salt
2 tsp dried shrimp paste, roasted and coarsely crushed · 1 tsp crushed coriander seeds

1. Prepare the chicken: In a large lidded pot fitted with a steamer insert large enough to accommodate the chicken completely, bring 2 inches of water to a boil. Tie the chicken legs together with a string and wrap the chicken with several layers of the banana leaves and greaseproof paper or foil. Place the chicken in the steamer insert, cover, and steam for 20 minutes. Discard the banana leaves and paper or foil, pat the chicken dry, and set aside.
2. Make the seasoning and stuffing: Preheat the oven to 350°F.
3. In a pan over medium heat, sauté all ingredients for 5 minutes, then let cool. Rub the outside of the chicken with the mixture. Fill the center of the chicken with the remaining mixture and wrap the chicken again in banana leaves, then greaseproof paper or foil. Place in a roasting pan and bake for 50 minutes, or until the meat is tender and falling off the bones. Remove from the oven and discard the banana leaves and paper or foil.
4. To serve, cut the chicken into pieces and arrange on a serving platter. Serve with the stuffing.

MEIXI LAKE
CHANGSHA, CHINA

DONG'AN VINEGAR CHICKEN

SERVES 6

2 Tbsp peanut oil · $^5/_8$ cup freshly grated ginger · 1 Tbsp dried red chili pepper
1 tsp whole Szechuan peppercorns · $3^1/_4$ cups mineral water · 1 whole ($2^1/_4$-lb) free-range chicken
$^5/_8$ cup local vinegar · 2 Tbsp salt · 1 tsp granulated sugar

1 In a large wok over medium-high heat, warm the oil. Add the ginger, chili pepper, and peppercorns and cook for 30 seconds to 1 minute, or until fragrant.

2 Transfer the contents of the wok to a large lidded pot over medium-high heat. Add the mineral water and bring to a boil. Add the whole chicken and braise for 10 minutes. Remove the chicken and cut into pieces; place the pieces in a large bowl and set aside.

3 Raise the heat to high and add the vinegar, salt, and sugar. Cook, stirring occasionally, for 5–10 minutes, or until the mixture thickens. Pour the contents of the pot over the chicken.

4 Prepare the chicken: In a large lidded pot fitted with a steamer insert large enough to accommodate the chicken completely, bring 1 inch of water to a boil. Place the chicken in the steamer insert, cover, and steam for 5 minutes (reserve the cooking liquid).

5 Place the chicken and the cooking liquid in a serving bowl and serve.

THE NAKA ISLAND
PHUKET, THAILAND

PLA NUENG MANOW (STEAMED FISH WITH LIME CHILI SAUCE)

SERVES 4

For the sea bass:
$2^1/_2$ lb whole baby sea bass · 1 oz lemongrass · Salt, to taste

For the lime chili sauce:
$^2/_3$ cup granulated sugar · $^1/_4$ cup freshly squeezed lime juice · $^1/_4$ cup fish sauce
5 cloves garlic · $^1/_2$ oz Thai red chili peppers

For serving:
4 cups white cabbage, blanched · 8 limes, sliced, for garnish
8 large red chili peppers, sliced, for garnish
$^1/_2$ bunch fresh cilantro, chopped, for garnish · 2 cups white jasmine rice, cooked

1. Prepare the sea bass: Season the sea bass with salt. Using the back of a knife, lightly crush the lemongrass.
2. In a large lidded pot fitted with a steamer insert large enough to accommodate the bass completely, bring 1 inch of water to a boil. Fold the lemongrass and place it in the steamer insert, then place the sea bass on top of it. Cover and steam for 10–15 minutes. Remove the bass from the steamer and set it aside on a plate. Discard the lemongrass.
3. Make the lime chili sauce: In a blender, combine all the ingredients and process until smooth.
4. To serve, arrange the cabbage on a serving platter and top with the sea bass. Pour the lime sauce over the fish and cabbage. Garnish with the sliced limes, chili peppers, and cilantro and serve with the rice.

“The combinations of the freshness, the unique spice, and the simplicity of this recipe represent Thailand; subtle but flourished, and always welcoming.”

NARUCHIT (SANK) RUGPHAT
sous chef, The Naka Island

THE PRINCE GALLERY TOKYO KIOICHO

TOKYO, JAPAN

CARPACCIO OF SEA BREAM AND SOBA WITH CAVIAR AND VEGETABLES

SERVES 4

For the vegetables:

2 broccoli florets · 2 cauliflower florets · 2 ears baby corn · 2 okra pods

For the soup stock:

1 Tbsp dried dashi (bonito fish soup) stock · 1/3 cup dark soy sauce
1/3 cup ponzu sauce · 1/3 cup mirin (sweet rice wine) · 2 1/2 Tbsp lemon-flavored olive oil
1 Tbsp minced onion · 1 Tbsp minced myoga (Japanese ginger) · 1 tsp wasabi

For the soba noodles:

3 1/2 oz soba noodles

For serving:

16 (10-oz or 1/2-inch-thick) slices sea bream · 4 cherry tomatoes, quartered, for garnish
2 cups microgreens, for garnish · 2 tsp caviar, for garnish · 4 thin slices radish, for garnish
4 thin slices sudachi (a sour citrus fruit similar to a lime), for garnish
Edible flowers, for garnish · Freshly ground black pepper, to taste

1. Prepare the vegetables: In a large pot over medium heat, bring 2 cups of water to a boil. Add the broccoli, cauliflower, baby corn, and okra and boil for about 3 minutes, or until softened. Drain the vegetables and cut them into pieces. Set aside.
2. Make the soup stock: In a large lidded pot over medium heat, combine the dashi, rice wine, and soy sauce with 2 cups of water and bring to a boil; set aside to cool.
3. Stir the ponzu sauce and oil into the soup stock, cover, and set aside.
4. Prepare the soba noodles: Wash the noodles in cold water. In a separate pot over high heat, bring 1 quart of water to a boil. Add the noodles and cook for 1 minute, then remove from the heat and drain into a colander.
5. Dip the noodles in the soup stock, then place them, in the shape of a bar, on a serving platter. Cut the noodles into 8 portions.
6. Add the onion, myoga, and wasabi to the soup stock. Dip the slices of sea bream into the stock.
7. To serve, season the sea bream with pepper. Cover the noodles with the slices of sea bream and garnish with the tomatoes, microgreens, caviar, radish, sudachi, and flowers. Serve with the soup stock.

Recipe by Ken Takahashi, executive chef, The Prince Gallery Tokyo Kioicho

THE ROYAL BEGONIA
SANYA HAITANG BAY, CHINA

TAMARIND POLYGONUM JUMBO SEAFOOD STEW WITH OKRA AND HAINANESE PINEAPPLE

SERVES 4

For the spice paste:
8 shallots, peeled and diced · 3 cloves garlic, peeled and diced
6 fresh red chili peppers, seeded and diced
8 dried red chili peppers, soaked, halved, seeded, and diced
1 stalk lemongrass, white part only, diced · 1 Tbsp peanut oil
1 tsp belacan (Malay shrimp paste) · 3/4 tsp ground turmeric

For the seafood stew:
2 Tbsp tamarind paste · 1 cup very hot water · 2 Tbsp peanut oil
2 cups room-temperature water · 2–3 tomatoes, quartered · 8 pieces okra
3 3/4 oz Hainanese pineapple, sliced · 2 sprigs polygonum leaves (Vietnamese coriander)
Salt, to taste · 11 oz Hainanese baby lobster · 6 1/2 oz codfish · 6–8 king prawns
3 3/4 oz squid, flower cut · 4 Hainanese jumbo clams · 4 fresh scallops
4 fresh mussels · 2 Tbsp coconut cream

1 Make the spice paste: Combine all the ingredients in a mortar and pestle or the bowl of a food processor fitted with the "S" blade or a in blender and grind or process into a paste. Set aside.

2 Make the seafood stew: Soak the tamarind paste in the very hot water for 15 minutes. Discard the seeds and pulp and reserve the juice.

3 In a frying pan over medium heat, warm the oil. Add the spice paste and fry for 3–4 minutes, or until fragrant. Add the room-temperature water and the tamarind juice, tomatoes, okra, pineapple, and polygonum leaves. Season with salt and bring to a boil. When the okra and tomatoes are almost cooked, reduce the heat to low and add the seafood. Simmer for 5 minutes, or until cooked. Remove from the heat.

4 To serve, stir in the coconut cream and serve hot.

Recipe by Bernard Yu, executive sous chef, The Royal Begonia

SHERATON GRANDE SUKHUMVIT
BANGKOK, THAILAND

KOY TUNA

SERVES 4

For the khao khua (toasted rice powder):
2½ Tbsp sticky rice

For the koy tuna:
12½ oz tuna loin, finely diced · 2½ Tbsp chili powder
2½ Tbsp Khao Khua (above) · 2 Tbsp fish sauce · 2 Tbsp freshly squeezed lime juice
1 shallot, peeled and minced · ⅝ cup chopped fresh sawtooth cilantro
½ cup julienned kaffir lime leaves · 2 scallions, sliced
3¾ oz red onion, sliced into 4 rings · 1 oz whole long beans, for garnish
1 cup fresh Thai basil, julienned, for garnish · 4 candied lemon wheels, for garnish
¼ cup chopped fresh mint, for garnish

1 Make the khao khua: In a dry pan over medium heat, toast the sticky rice grains for 8–10 minutes, or until fragrant. Remove from the heat and transfer to a mortar and pestle or the bowl of a food processor fitted with the "S" blade. Pound or process into a fine powder.

2 Make the koy tuna: In a large bowl, combine the tuna, chili powder, and khao khua and toss until the tuna is coated. Add the fish sauce and lime juice and toss together gently. Add the shallot, cilantro, lime leaves, and scallions and toss gently. Form into four equal-size quenelles (elegant oval scoops).

3 To serve, place a slice of onion on four serving plates. Arrange one quenelle on each slice. Garnish with the beans, basil, and mint, and a slice of candied lemon and serve.

MANACHAI KONKANGPLU

executive chef at the Sheraton Grande Sukhumvit, Bangkok, Thailand

YOUR FAVORITE LOCAL PLACE TO EAT?

Bang Pu in Samut Prakan province, just outside Bangkok. The area of mud flats and mangrove forests is owned and managed by the Thai military and at first seems a strange place to go, but there are many restaurants on stilts here serving incredible Thai seafood dishes. It gets very busy on weekends.

WHAT DO YOU ORDER THERE?

Poo pad pong karee—stir-fried crab with egg and curry powder. It's a luxurious and delicious Thai seafood dish everyone should try.

YOUR FAVORITE INGREDIENT TO USE IN COOKING?

I am Thai, so it is chili! It is the spice of our life and we eat it every day and at every meal!

YOUR PREFERRED TRAVEL DESTINATION FOR AN EPICUREAN EXPERIENCE?

A day traveling along the Chao Phraya River exploring unseen neighborhoods and discovering small family restaurants.

YOUR PREFERRED COMFORT FOOD?

To me, comfort food is simple food, such as chili dip and vegetables, prepared with love and shared with friends.

SOFÍA SANCHEZ DE BETAK

art director and founder, UnderOurSky.com

YOUR FAVORITE LOCAL PLACE TO EAT?

Matsudaya Sushi in Gion.

YOUR BEST MEAL THERE?

Sushi omakase.

THE BEST SPOT FOR A COCKTAIL?

Midnight Cafe 528 (GO.NI.HACHI), Gion.

WHAT DO YOU ORDER THERE?

Japanese whiskey on the rocks.

FAVORITE INGREDIENT IN A DISH?

Ponzu sauce.

YOUR FAVORITE FOOD AND DRINK PAIRING?

Sushi and dry cold sake.

THE BEST QUALITY ABOUT THE LOCAL CUISINE?

The delicate way they cut the fish and how it holds its texture when it's so fresh.

WHAT DISH REMINDS YOU OF HOME?

Asado, Argentinean barbecue.

YOUR PREFERRED COMFORT FOOD?

Dulce de leche.

SUIRAN
KYOTO, JAPAN

FOIE GRAS MARINATED IN JAPANESE SAKE LEES

SERVES 9

For the foie gras:
$1^{2}/_{3}$ cups milk · 2 tsp salt, divided · 1 pinch freshly ground black pepper
11 oz foie gras · 2 cups plus $1^{1}/_{2}$ Tbsp sake lees · Fleur de sel, for serving

For the crumbles:
$3^{1}/_{2}$ Tbsp unsalted butter, room temperature · $^{1}/_{2}$ cup all-purpose flour
$^{1}/_{4}$ cup granulated sugar · $^{1}/_{4}$ cup pine nuts (pignolis)

1 Prepare the foie gras: In a mixing bowl, combine the milk, pepper, and 1 tsp of the salt with ⅞ cup of water. Add the foie gras and marinate in the refrigerator for 2 hours.

2 Strain the foie gras mixture and discard the soaking liquid. Place the foie gras in a vacuum-seal bag. Using a candy thermometer, bring a pot of water over high heat to 145°F. Add the sealed bag of foie gras to the pot and cook for 35 minutes. Remove the bag from the pot.

3 Trim all the fat from the foie gras. Season it with the remaining 1 tsp of salt and place it in a sealable plastic bag with the sake lees. Refrigerate for at least 5 days.

4 Make the crumbles: Preheat the oven to 320°F. Line a baking sheet with parchment paper.

5 Using a stand mixer fitted with the paddle attachment, beat the butter until lightened. Add the flour and sugar and beat until well combined. Add the pine nuts and mix together.

6 Spread the dough onto a baking sheet. Bake for 8 minutes, then set aside to cool completely.

7 To serve, rinse the sake lees off the foie gras and dice it. Crumble the baked dough. Arrange the foie gras on a platter and sprinkle with the fleur de sel. Serve with the crumbles.

Recipe by Yoshio Matsuse, executive chef, Suiran

TWELVE AT HENGSHAN
SHANGHAI, CHINA

TASTE OF SHANGHAI

SERVES 4

For the hairy crab jelly (makes 4 oz):
2 oz hairy crab meat, roe removed and discarded · 1 Tbsp olive oil · 2 Tbsp heavy cream
1 oz liquid fruit pectin · Salt and freshly ground black pepper, to taste

For the pumpkin puree (makes 4 oz):
4 oz fresh pumpkin, peeled, seeded, and diced · 1 pinch salt

For the green onion pancakes (makes 8):
1 cup all-purpose flour · 1/2 cup pork fat · 1/2 cup chopped scallions
1/2 Tbsp salt · 1/4 cup vegetable oil

For the Taste of Shanghai:
1/2 cup freshly shredded Parmesan cheese · 4 radishes, sliced · 4 baby carrots, sliced
4 snow peas, sliced · 2 baby zucchinis, sliced · 1 (16-oz) rock lobster, steamed, tail removed
8 Green Onion Pancakes (above) · 4 oz Hairy Crab Jelly (above)
4 oz Pumpkin Puree (above) · 2 oz fresh strawberries, sliced, for garnish
2 oz fresh cherry tomatoes, halved, for garnish
2 oz white truffles, shaved, for garnish
Salt and freshly ground black pepper, to taste

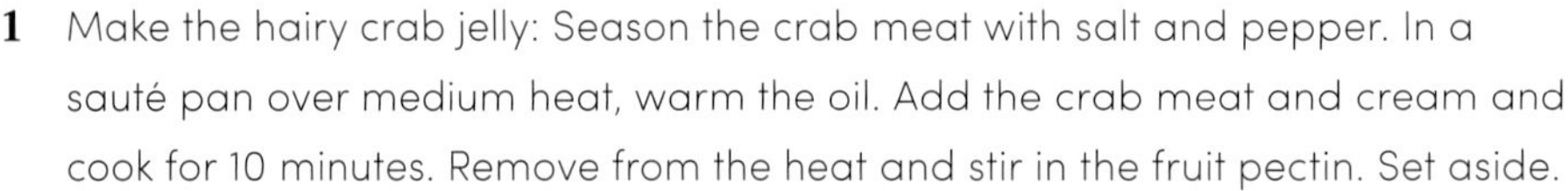

1. Make the hairy crab jelly: Season the crab meat with salt and pepper. In a sauté pan over medium heat, warm the oil. Add the crab meat and cream and cook for 10 minutes. Remove from the heat and stir in the fruit pectin. Set aside.
2. Make the pumpkin puree: Place the pumpkin in a saucepan over medium heat. Season with the salt and cook for 20 minutes, or until tender. Remove from the heat and use an immersion blender to puree until smooth.
3. Make the green onion pancakes: In a mixing bowl, thoroughly combine the flour, pork fat, scallions, and salt. In a large frying pan over medium heat, warm the oil. Using a spoon, drop half the batter in four separate scoops into the pan and cook for 5 minutes on each side. Transfer the pancakes to a plate and cover with foil to keep warm. Repeat with the remaining batter.
4. Make the Taste of Shanghai: In a frying pan over medium heat, arrange the shredded Parmesan into four small circles and cook for 5 minutes, or until crispy. Remove from the heat.
5. Prepare the vegetables: In a lidded pot fitted with a steamer insert, bring 1 inch of water to a boil. Place the radishes, carrots, peas, and zucchinis in the steamer insert, season with salt and pepper, cover, and steam for 3 minutes. Remove from the heat.
6. To serve, arrange the steamed vegetables on a serving platter. Arrange the lobster, green onion pancakes, jelly, puree, and Parmesan crisps on top of the vegetables. Garnish with the strawberries, tomatoes, and truffles, season with salt and pepper, and serve.

VANA BELLE
KOH SAMUI, THAILAND

MIANG KHAM ONE-BITE WRAPS WITH SWEET AND SOUR TAMARIND SAUCE

SERVES 4

For the wraps:
1 lime, diced · 1/2 cup peeled and finely diced fresh ginger
1/2 cup dried coconut flakes, toasted · 3/8 cup chopped roasted peanuts
1/3 cup finely chopped red onion · 1/3 cup finely chopped bird's eye chili pepper
1/4 cup dried shrimp · 16 fresh betel leaves, washed and patted dry

For the sweet and sour tamarind sauce:
3 1/4 cups tamarind juice · 2 cups palm sugar · 1/2 cup dried shrimp · 2 Tbsp shrimp paste
1 1/3 cups dried coconut flakes, toasted · 2 Tbsp finely chopped fresh galangal root
1/4 cup peeled and finely chopped fresh ginger · 2 Tbsp finely chopped fresh lemongrass

1 Prepare the wraps: Arrange the ingredients for the wraps, except the betel leaves, in individual bowls on a large serving platter. Place the betel leaves around the edge of the platter in a decorative flower shape.

2 Make the sauce: In a saucepan over medium heat, combine the tamarind juice, palm sugar, dried shrimp, and shrimp paste and slowly bring to a boil. Stir well until the palm sugar and shrimp paste have fully dissolved. Reduce the heat to low and add the remaining ingredients. Simmer for 1–2 minutes, or until the sauce thickens. Transfer the sauce to a bowl. Refrigerate until ready to use.

3 To eat, place a leaf in the palm of your hand and make a cone shape. Add a small amount of each ingredient to the center of the leaf. Top with a small spoonful of the tamarind sauce. Gather the corners of the leaf together to form a wrap and eat in a single bite.

Recipe by Nattanan Deeruang, executive chef, Vana Belle

EUROPE

Dolmadakia (Stuffed Grape Leaves)
Blue Palace, Crete

Recipe on page 77

AUGUSTINE
PRAGUE, CZECH REPULIC

AUGUSTINE SECRET

SERVES 1

For the vanilla-cinnamon syrup (makes 4¼ cups):
2 vanilla beans, split and seeded · 3 cinnamon sticks

For the orange foam:
1 egg white · 2 dashes orange bitters · ⅜ cup freshly squeezed orange juice

For the Augustine Secret:
1½ oz Becherovka (a Czech herbal liqueur)
⅔ oz Vanilla-Cinnamon Syrup (above) · ⅔ oz freshly squeezed lemon juice
1 dash chocolate bitters · 1 dollop Orange Foam (above), for topping

1 Make the vanilla-cinnamon syrup: In a saucepan, combine the vanilla bean seeds and cinnamon sticks with 4¼ cups of water and bring to a boil for 2–3 minutes.

2 Make the orange foam: Combine all the ingredients with ⅞ cup of water in a cream whipper or siphon charged with carbon dioxide and refrigerate for 30 minutes.

3 Make the cocktail: Fill a cocktail shaker ¾ full with cubed ice. Add the Becherovka, vanilla-cinnamon syrup, lemon juice, and chocolate bitters and shake vigorously until cold. Strain into a martini glass, top off with the orange foam, and serve.

Recipe by Svetlana Persova, food and beverage manager, Augustine

BLUE PALACE
CRETE, GREECE

DOLMADAKIA
(STUFFED GRAPE LEAVES)

SERVES 4

$^2/_3$ cup chopped tomatoes · 5 cups white long-grain rice
1 medium onion, finely chopped · $1^1/_4$ cups finely chopped scallions
$^3/_4$ cup grated zucchini · $^2/_3$ cup grated carrots · $^1/_2$ cup grated potatoes
$^1/_4$ cup finely chopped fresh dill · $^1/_4$ cup finely chopped fresh mint
1 tsp salt · $^1/_2$ tsp freshly ground black pepper · $^5/_8$ cup extra-virgin olive oil, divided
40 medium-sized, tender grape leaves, washed · $^1/_4$ cup sliced carrots
$^1/_2$ cup finely chopped dried onion · $^1/_4$ cup plus 3 Tbsp freshly squeezed lemon juice

1 Place the chopped tomatoes in a blender and blend until smooth.

2 In a mixing bowl, combine the tomatoes, rice, onion, scallions, zucchini, carrots, potatoes, dill, mint, salt, pepper, and ¼ cup plus 3 Tbsp of the oil. Add 2 cups of water and mix thoroughly with your hands.

3 Remove the stems from the grape leaves. Place 1 Tbsp of the filling in the center of each leaf. Fold the bottom left corner of the leaf over the filling, followed by the bottom right corner. Roll the wrapped filling forward over the rest of the leaf.

4 At the bottom of a large saucepan, place the sliced carrots and dried onion in a layer (they will protect the stuffed rolls from burning). Place the stuffed rolls on top of the carrots and dried onion, side by side, in layers. Place an upside-down plate on top of the upper layer and fill the pan with cold water. Place over medium heat and cook for 40 minutes. Five minutes before removing from the heat, add the remaining oil and the lemon juice. Remove from the heat and serve.

"An authentic Greek recipe with a Cretan twist, utilizing the island's most unique ingredients; the aromatic herbs, the fresh vegetables, and the pure olive oil–a pillar of the Cretan gastronomy."

ALEXANDROS LEFKADITIS
executive chef, Blue Palace

BLUE PALACE
CRETE, GREECE

CRETAN FEAST

The most famous celebrations in Greece are the festivals to honor the saint-protector of each village. In Crete, locals gather to enjoy homegrown food and recite the famous *mantinades*, improvised rhymes to celebrate occasions such as love, life, or friendship, and everyone sings and dances into the small hours of the night. Guests can get acquainted with the island's cultural and gastronomical traditions through this unique ritual.

Large bonfires are lit at Blue Palace's private beach for the cooking of the famous Antikristo lamb, sprinkled in sea salt and slowly cooked over the fire for five hours. Authentic local delicacies are prepared on-site to the distinct tunes of the Cretan lyra, all in a seaside landscape of spectacular beauty.

Enjoy authentic local delicacies served family-style.
Opposite: The Blue Door Taverna, setting for the feast.

CARESSE
BODRUM, TURKEY

BLACK ISLAND MOUSSE

SERVES 4

For the black island mousse:
7 oz bittersweet chocolate, chopped · 2 sheets gelatin · 2 Tbsp heavy cream
5 large egg yolks · 2 Tbsp plus 1 tsp granulated sugar

For the tangerine puree:
Freshly squeezed juice of 2 medium tangerines
1 Tbsp granulated sugar · 1 Tbsp cornstarch

For the hazelnut-chocolate ganache:
$3\frac{1}{2}$ oz bittersweet chocolate, chopped · 7 Tbsp heavy cream
$\frac{2}{3}$ oz hazelnuts, crushed · Nutella, for serving

1 Make the mousse: Melt the chocolate using the double-boiler technique—Place 1 inch of water in a saucepan over medium-low heat and bring to a gentle simmer. Place a medium heatproof mixing bowl on top of the saucepan, making sure the bowl does not touch the water, and add the bitter chocolate to the glass bowl. Stir until the chocolate is just melted; remove from the heat.

2 Soften the gelatin sheets by placing them in a bowl of cold water for 5–10 minutes. Remove them from the water, place them in a microwavable bowl, and microwave at 50 percent power in 30-second intervals, stirring after each interval, or until the gelatin is melted. Set aside.

3 In a small bowl, whisk the cream until foamy. In a separate bowl, whisk together the egg yolks and sugar until foamy. Combine the cream and the egg mixture, then gradually (in thirds) stir in the melted chocolate. Add the melted gelatin and stir to combine. Transfer the mixture to four bowl-shaped plastic cups (each should be about half full) and place them in the freezer for at least 20 minutes.

4 Make the puree: In a mixing bowl, combine the tangerine juice, sugar, and cornstarch and whisk until smooth.

5 Make the ganache: Place the chocolate in a medium mixing bowl. Place the cream in a small saucepan over medium-high heat. Heat for 3–4 minutes, or until a skin begins to form on the cream. Pour the hot cream over the chocolate. Set aside for 1 minute to allow the chocolate to begin to melt.

6 Whisk the mixture vigorously, or until smooth and the chocolate has melted. Stir in the hazelnuts. Cover with plastic wrap and set aside to cool to room temperature. Whisk the cooled ganache until lightened.

7 To serve, invert the cups onto serving plates to unmold the frozen mousse. Top the mousse with the puree, then pour the ganache over the puree. Decorate the plates as desired with the Nutella.

CARESSE
BODRUM, TURKEY

TANGERINE HARVESTING

The concierge team leads guests to tangerine gardens in small Turkish villages with curved narrow roads and thousands of layers of green and blue landscape in between. Following hundreds of years of tradition, guests hand-pick the fruits from the trees and gather them in handmade baskets.

While all are enjoying the unique scents and natural scenery of the lush gardens, Caresse's butlers prepare a picnic with local delicacies, to be enjoyed alfresco. Back at the resort, Caresse's executive chef offers a private class to prepare the restaurant's signature tangerine jam, which guests can enjoy at breakfast the following morning.

Left: Freshly picked tangerines.
Above: Caresse's signature Satsuma cocktail.

CASTILLO HOTEL SON VIDA

MALLORCA, SPAIN

GRILLED SEA BASS WITH NORI ALGAE AIOLI AND PEPPERS

SERVES 4

½ cup granulated sugar · 1 red bell pepper, cut into strips
1 fresh red chili pepper, chopped · 1 sheet nori algae
5 Tbsp plus 1 tsp extra-virgin olive oil, divided · 1⅓ lb sea bass fillets
⅞ cup whole milk · 1 small clove garlic · 1 piece bok choy, steamed, for garnish
Red sprouts, for garnish · Salt and freshly ground black pepper, to taste

1. In a small saucepan over medium heat, combine the sugar with ¼ cup plus 3 Tbsp of water. Cook, stirring, until the sugar is dissolved. Set aside to cool.
2. Place the bell pepper strips and chili pepper in a bowl with the sugar-and-water mixture, cover, and set aside for 24 hours.
3. Place the nori algae in a pan with 2 Tbsp of the oil over low heat. Using a candy thermometer, maintain a temperature of 150°F in the oil and algae mixture for 10 minutes. Set aside to cool to room temperature.
4. Preheat the oven to 350°F.
5. In a large oven-safe frying pan or skillet over medium-high heat, warm 1 tsp of the oil. Add the fillets to the pan and fry them on each side for about 5 minutes. Place the pan in the oven for 10–12 minutes.

6. In a blender, combine the remaining 3 Tbsp of oil with the milk, garlic, and nori algae. Season with salt and pepper and blend until the mixture thickens slightly.
7. Remove the peppers from the sugar-and-water mixture, rinse them, and transfer them to a sauté pan over medium heat. Season with salt and sauté for 2 minutes.
8. Place the peppers on serving plates. Place the fillets on the peppers. Surround with nori algae aioli and garnish with the bok choy and sprouts. Serve.

CONVENTO DO ESPINHEIRO

ÉVORA, PORTUGAL

SERICÁ

SERVES 6

1½ cups granulated sugar · 6 large eggs, separated
⅓ cup all-purpose flour · 2 cups whole milk · 1 cinnamon stick
Fresh peel of ½ a lemon · Ground cinnamon, for sprinkling

1 In a large mixing bowl, combine the sugar and egg yolks and beat until creamy.

2 Dissolve the flour in the milk.

3 In a large, deep saucepan over low heat, combine the milk mixture, egg yolk mixture, cinnamon stick, and lemon peel. Bring to a boil and immediately remove from the heat. Set aside to cool to room temperature.

4 Preheat the oven to 320°F.

5 Discard the cinnamon stick and lemon peel.

6 In a large mixing bowl, beat the egg whites until foamy. Gradually fold them into the cooled mixture.

7 Transfer to a baking dish and sprinkle with the ground cinnamon. Bake for 35 minutes, or until golden on top. Remove from the oven, dust with the cinnamon, and serve.

CRISTALLO

CORTINA D'AMPEZZO, ITALY

TERRA

SERVES 4

10 oz whole wheat spaghetti · 1²/₃ cups beet juice · ¹/₂ cup raspberry vinegar
5 oz South Tyrolean speck, sliced into small pieces · ³/₄ cup plus 4 tsp heavy cream
3³/₄ oz Blu di Capra (goat's milk Gorgonzola cheese), crumbled
¹/₄ cup freshly grated horseradish

1. In a large pot over medium heat, bring 1 gallon of salted water to a boil. Add the spaghetti and boil for 5 minutes. Drain, then transfer the spaghetti to a large saucepan.
2. Add the beet juice and vinegar to the saucepan and cook over low heat for 5 minutes, or until al dente. Immediately transfer the spaghetti to a warmed platter and cover with foil. Reserve the cooking liquid.
3. In a sauté pan over low heat, add the speck and sauté for 2–3 minutes, or until crisp. Remove from the heat and set aside.
4. In a saucepan over medium heat, cook the cream until it is reduced to one-third of its volume, 5–6 minutes. Remove from the heat. Add the cheese and horseradish and stir to combine.
5. To serve, add the reserved cooking liquid, cream sauce, and speck to the spaghetti.

Recipe by Fabrizio Albini, executive chef, Cristallo

EXCELSIOR HOTEL GALLIA

MILAN, ITALY

LINGUINE WITH TURBOT CARBONARA SAUCE AND ALMOND CREAM

SERVES 4

For the fish stock (makes 5 oz):

1/4 cup extra-virgin olive oil · 7 oz whitefish bones · 1 white onion, peeled and chopped
1 stalk celery, chopped · 1/2 leek, chopped · 1/2 stalk fennel, chopped
Salt and freshly ground black pepper, to taste

For the almond cream:

3 1/2 oz almonds, chopped

For the carbonara sauce and linguine:

7/8 cup heavy cream · 3 1/2 oz bacon · 5 oz Fish Stock (above) · 8 1/2 oz dried linguine
5 1/2 oz ground raw turbot flesh · 6 large egg yolks · 2 oz whole cherry tomatoes
1 recipe Almond Cream (above) · Dill sprouts, for garnish · Salt and freshly ground black pepper, to taste

1 Make the fish stock: In a heavy pot over medium-high heat, warm the oil. Add the fish bones and vegetables and cook for 5 minutes. Season with salt and pepper, add just enough water to cover all ingredients, and cook for 20 minutes. Remove from the heat and leave in the pot for 1 hour to allow the flavors to infuse. Strain out the bones and vegetables and reserve the liquid, seasoning again with salt, if needed.

2 Make the almond cream: In a blender, add the almonds and ½ cup of water. Blend, then strain the into a measuring cup, discarding the solids. Set aside.

3 Prepare the linguine: In a medium saucepan over medium heat, bring the heavy cream and bacon to a boil. Cook for 1 hour. Strain, reserving the liquid.

4 In a large saucepan over medium heat, combine the reserved bacon cream with the fish stock.

5 Cook the linguine according to the package directions to al dente. Strain and transfer the cooked pasta to the saucepan containing the fish stock mixture. Cook for 2 minutes. Add the turbot, egg yolks, tomatoes, and almon cream. Season with salt and pepper. Cook for 1–2 minutes, then remove from the heat.

6 To serve, transfer the warm sauce to a shallow platter. Place the cooked pasta on top and garnish with dill sprouts. Serve hot.

Recipe by Vincenzo and Antonio Lebano, chefs, Excelsior Hotel Gallia

MARGHERITA MACCAPANI MISSONI

fashion designer, model, and actress

YOUR FAVORITE LOCAL PLACE TO EAT?

La Latteria di San Marco, Milan.

YOUR BEST MEAL THERE?

Bulgur alla crudaiola, a secret recipe of finely chopped salad, carrots, tomatoes, and basil.

YOUR FAVORITE INGREDIENT IN A DISH?

Persimmon.

WHAT DISH WILL YOU TRAVEL ACROSS THE WORLD TO EAT?

Mint chocolate chip smoothie from Café Gratitude in LA.

YOUR FAVORITE FOOD AND DRINK PAIRING?

Fresh sea urchins with dry white wine.

THE BEST QUALITY ABOUT THE LOCAL CUISINE?

Discovering vegetables I've never tasted before.

YOUR PREFERRED TRAVEL DESTINATION FOR AN EPICUREAN EXPERIENCE?

A weekend in Cadaqués with a dinner at El Celler de Can Roca, Girona.

WHAT DISH REMINDS YOU OF HOME?

Vitello tonnato.

YOUR PREFERRED COMFORT FOOD?

Palatschinken suppe.

FALISIA
DUINO-AURISINA, ITALY

LA FALISIA

SERVES 1

1 Tbsp maraschino liqueur · 1 tsp lychee liqueur · 3–4 strawberries or raspberries
$3^1/_3$ oz champagne, for topping off · Mint leaves, for garnish

1 In a white wine glass, combine the maraschino and lychee liqueurs with the berries.

2 Top off with the champagne, garnish with the mint, and serve.

GRAND HOTEL RIVER PARK
BRATISLAVA, SLOVAKIA

PRESSBURG SOUR

SERVES 1

2 raspberries · 2 blackberries · 1 tsp granulated sugar
1½ oz Borovička (a juniper brandy; similar to dry gin) · 2 Tbsp lime juice
1 Tbsp honey · 1 tsp berry jam · Club soda, for topping off

1 Muddle the berries with the sugar and place them in the serving glass.

2 Add the Borovička, lime juice, honey, and berry jam and stir to combine. Top off with the club soda and crushed ice and serve.

Recipe by Samuel Kozik, head bartender, Grand Hotel River Park

THE GRITTI PALACE
VENICE, ITALY

GOBY FISH RISOTTO

SERVES 4

For the goby broth:
2 lb goby fish · 3/8 cup extra-virgin olive oil · 1/4 cup julienned leek
1/3 stalk celery, diced · 3 Tbsp diced white onion · 1 shallot, peeled and diced
1 clove garlic, peeled · 1/4 cup plus 2 Tbsp white wine · 2 bay leaves

For the risotto:
1 3/4 oz red bell peppers, for garnish · 1 3/4 oz yellow bell peppers, for garnish
1/3 cup julienned fresh basil · 4 Tbsp extra-virgin olive oil, divided
10 oz Vialone Nano rice · 3 1/2 Tbsp white wine · 2 tsp unsalted butter
3/4 cup minced fresh parsley, for garnish · Salt and white pepper, to taste

1. Make the goby broth: Remove the head and entrails of the fish; rinse the body well inside and out.
2. In a sauté pan over medium heat, warm the oil. Add the leek, celery, onion, shallot, and garlic and sauté for 8 minutes, or until browned. Add the fish and sauté for 4 minutes. Add the wine and simmer for about 3 minutes, or until most of the moisture evaporates. Add the bay leaves and enough water to cover the fish by 2 inches; simmer for 45 minutes. Discard the bay leaves.
3. Filter the broth through a large sieve, then through a vegetable mill, and finally through a fine-mesh sieve or chinois. Transfer the broth to a clean saucepan and place over low heat.
4. Make the risotto: Preheat the oven to 475°F. Line a baking sheet with parchment paper.
5. Place the bell peppers on the baking sheet and roast for 8 minutes, or until the skin is charred. Transfer them to a sealed container and set aside for 30 minutes.
6. Remove the peppers from the container, peel off the skin, and toss them with the basil and season with salt and pepper. Cut them into small rounds and set aside.
7. In a saucepan over medium-high heat, warm 3 Tbsp of the oil. Add the rice and toast for 2 minutes, stirring occasionally. Add the wine and simmer for about 2 minutes, or until most of the moisture evaporates. Add a ladleful of the goby broth and simmer for about 3 minutes, stirring occasionally, or until most of the moisture evaporates. Continue to add the broth, 1 ladleful at a time, and simmer for 2–3 minutes after each addition, stirring occasionally, or until most of the moisture evaporates and the rice is cooked. The grains of rice should be a little firm in the middle. Remove from the heat, add the butter, and stir until fully incorporated.
8. Transfer the risotto to a serving bowl. Drizzle with the remaining 1 Tbsp of oil and scatter the parsley over the top. Season with additional white pepper, garnish with the pepper rounds, and serve.

Recipe by Daniele Turco, executive chef, Club del Doge Restaurant, The Gritti Palace

DANIELE TURCO

executive chef at The Gritti Palace, Venice, Italy

THE BEST SPOT FOR A COCKTAIL?

Personally, I like Harry's Bar, which, like The Gritti Palace, is a legend in Venice.

WHAT MAKES THE SETTING MEMORABLE?

Harry's has a really special atmosphere to it—if only the walls could talk!—and the people there make the difference. The Bellini cocktails made with fresh peaches and the martinis are some of the best in town, together with the iconic Bellini cocktail served at the Bar Longhi, the elegant and refined bar at The Gritti Palace.

YOUR FAVORITE INGREDIENT TO USE IN COOKING?

Fresh langoustines.

IN WHICH RECIPES DOES THIS INGREDIENT WORK BEST?

I like to use them for special starters and in soups and risottos, like the Hemingway Risotto, the signature dish of the Club del Doge restaurant.

WHAT IS A DISH NO ONE SHOULD VISIT THIS CITY WITHOUT EATING?

Everyone should taste our Venetian cicchetti, similar to tapas, or local specialties such as Venetian-style liver and sarde in saor (sweet-and-sour sardines).

CULINARY COURSES AT THE

GRITTI EPICUREAN SCHOOL

Under the tutelage of executive chef Daniele Turco, guests will learn how to prepare an exquisite three-course dinner using local Venetian ingredients including fresh fish, vegetables, and homemade pasta, and completed with wine pairings and a delicious dessert. Depending on the experience chosen, guests may begin the day with a tour of the Rialto Market—one of the oldest in Italy—accompanied by the chef, where they will learn more about local products, seasonality, and how to select ingredients, followed by a typical Venetian *aperitivo* with *cicchetti* (small side dishes) at a traditional *bacaro* (gastropub), before beginning the cooking course. Guests may also opt for an exclusive wine tasting led by The Gritti Palace's head sommelier, Sandro, in which they will learn about different wine regions and taste some of Italy's finest wines.

Pasta and fresh ingredients waiting to be used in chef Daniele Turco's Venetian dishes in the Epicurean School kitchen.

HOTEL ALFONSO XIII

SEVILLE, SPAIN

TAPAS TASTING TOUR

Seville has one of the highest ratios in the world of bars to people, and knowing exactly where to go for the best, freshest, and most authentic tapas is a mixture of luck and know-how. Appreciate an afternoon or night of tapas in Seville like a local, led by the hotel's friendly and knowledgeable Andalusian guides, with visits to up to five tapas bars. Sun, siesta, and sangria may be the typical Spanish cliché, but Hotel Alfonso's tour goes beyond the typical. From extra-tender beef cheek to specialties at unassuming *abacerías* (grocery stores) with their walls lined with conserves, the tapas tasting tour changes every day but always features a range of chic traditional and avant-garde spots. Diners should come thirsty, too, as each tapa is paired with the perfect pour, from sherry to local whites and reds.

The tour allows guests to see the sights all around Seville, such as La Giralda bell tower and the Plaza de toros de la Real Maestranza de Caballería de Sevilla, Seville's bullring.

HOTEL ALFONSO XIII

SEVILLE, SPAIN

TORRIJAS
(SEVILLE FRENCH TOAST)

SERVES 5

1 quart sheep's milk · 1½ cups honey, plus more for serving
1 handful cloves · 1 loaf brioche, thickly sliced · 4¼ cups white wine
4 large eggs · 4¼ cups extra-virgin olive oil

1 In a large saucepan over medium heat, combine the sheep's milk, honey, cloves, and 1 cup of water and bring to a boil. Reduce the heat to low and simmer for 10 minutes, or until the honey is diluted and the mixture is well blended. Remove from the heat.

2 In a wide, deep bowl, combine the wine with 1 cup of water. In a separate wide, deep bowl, beat the eggs with a fork.

3 In a frying pan over medium-high heat, warm the oil. Steep 1 slice of the brioche first in the wine mixture, then in the eggs. Shake lightly to remove excess moisture and place in the frying pan. Cook until golden on each side and transfer to a platter to cool slightly. Repeat with the remaining slices.

4 One at a time, transfer the cooled slices to the milk mixture and soak for 2–3 minutes. Remove and set aside to cool completely before serving.

5 Serve with extra honey on the side.

HOTEL BRISTOL
VIENNA, AUSTRIA

BRISTOL ROYAL

SERVES 1

2/3 oz cherry liqueur · 1 oz Boiron Black cherry puree
1/3 oz almond syrup · 1/2 oz freshly squeezed lime juice
Bründlmayer Brut (a German sparkling wine), for topping off

1 In a cocktail shaker filled with ice, combine the cherry liqueur, cherry puree, almond syrup, and lime juice. Shake well and strain into a chilled champagne glass.

2 Top off with the Bründlmayer Brut and serve.

HOTEL BRISTOL
WARSAW, POLAND

SIGNATURE WHITE CHOCOLATE AND VANILLA CHEESECAKE

SERVES 8

For the crust:
½ cup (1 stick) unsalted butter, cubed and very cold · 1 egg yolk
¼ cup granulated sugar · 1 cup plus 2 Tbsp all-purpose flour

For the filling:
2 (8-oz) packages cream cheese, softened · ⅓ cup granulated sugar
3 large eggs · 2 Tbsp 2% milk · 1 vanilla bean, split and seeded
10 oz white chocolate, melted · 3¾ oz Polish prunes

1. Make the crust: Preheat the oven to 350°F.
2. In a mixing bowl, combine the sugar and egg yolk, then cut in the cold butter using a fork or pastry cutter. Add the flour and stir until well combined.
3. Dust a clean work surface with flour and turn out the dough onto the surface. Sprinkle a little more flour on top of the dough and roll it out into a 9-inch circle. Place it in an 8-inch springform pan.
4. Bake for 15–20 minutes, or until golden. Remove from the oven and set aside to cool.
5. Make the filling: Preheat the oven to 300°F. Tightly wrap the bottom and sides of the cooled springform pan containing the prebaked crust with aluminum foil until watertight.
6. In a mixing bowl, combine the cream cheese, sugar, eggs, milk, and vanilla bean seeds. Using a hand mixer, beat the mixture until well combined. Pour the melted white chocolate into the mixture and beat again just until well combined.
7. Pour the filling into the springform pan on top of the crust. Press the prunes into the batter.
8. Make a bain-marie (water bath): Fill a large roasting pan with about 1 inch of boiling water. Place the watertight springform pan in the roasting pan and bake for 50–60 minutes. Remove from the oven and set aside to cool completely on a rack.
9. Carefully remove the cake from the springform pan and serve.

HOTEL CALA DI VOLPE

PORTO CERVO, ITALY

YELLOW AND BLACK TAGLIOLINI WITH PRAWNS AND OVULI MUSHROOMS

SERVES 4

For the yellow pasta dough:
1 cup plus 3 Tbsp semolina flour · 3/4 cup plus 1 Tbsp all-purpose flour
3 large eggs · 1 large egg yolk · 30 saffron threads

For the black pasta dough:
1 cup plus 3 Tbsp semolina flour · 3/4 cup plus 1 Tbsp all-purpose flour
3 large eggs · 1 large egg yolk · 1 1/2 Tbsp squid ink

For the sauce:
20 fresh prawns, washed and patted dry · 3/4 cup extra-virgin olive oil, divided
2 cloves garlic, chopped, divided · 1 cup vegetable broth
7 oz fresh tomatoes, cut into strips · 1 dash salt
15 oz ovuli mushrooms, washed, patted dry, and thinly sliced, divided
1 cup chopped fresh parsley, divided

1. Make the yellow and black pastas: In two separate bowls, one for each color of pasta, mix the flours, the eggs, and the egg yolks. To the yellow dough bowl, add the saffron; to the black dough bowl, add the squid ink. Work the two doughs separately into balls until they are firm and evenly colored.
2. Stretch each of the dough balls into thin layers and run each layer through a pasta machine to make the tagliolini. Hang the pasta to dry in a dry place.
3. Make the sauce: Shell and remove the heads from eight of the prawns; cut them into pieces. Remove the heads from eight more of the prawns; keep the shells intact. Keep the last four prawns whole.
4. In a small bowl, combine ¼ cup of the oil and half of the garlic. Set aside.
5. In a large saucepan over medium heat, warm the remaining ½ cup of oil and the remaining garlic. Add all the prawns and the vegetable broth and cook for 2–3 minutes, or until browned. Add the tomatoes and salt and cook for 5 minutes. Add all but eight slices of the mushrooms and cook for 3 minutes. Add 2 Tbsp of the oil-and-garlic mixture and cook for 2 minutes. Add most of the parsley and cook for 2 minutes, or until the sauce has thickened. Remove from the heat.
6. Bring a large pot of salted water to a boil. Add the pasta and cook for 4–5 minutes. Remove from the heat. Drain the pasta through a colander and add it to the saucepan with the sauce; stir until the pasta is well coated.
7. Transfer to a large serving bowl and pour the remaining 2 Tbsp of the oil-and-garlic mixture over the dish. Garnish with the four whole prawns, reserved raw mushrooms, and remaining parsley; serve hot.

Recipe by Maurizio Locatelli, executive chef, Hotel Cala di Volpe

HOTEL DANIELI
VENICE, ITALY

CANNOLI OF CREAMED CODFISH WITH SPRITZ JELLY, GREEN OLIVE CAVIAR, CANDIED ORANGE, AND RICOTTA AND SAFFRON CREAM

SERVES 4

14½ oz soaked dried codfish · 1 quart whole milk · 1 shallot, peeled and chopped
5 bay leaves · 1¼ oz anchovies in oil, minced · 1¾ cups peanut oil · 10 oz Aperol
2 Tbsp granulated sugar · 2 tsp agar · 7 oz ricotta cheese · ½ cup chopped fresh chives
¼ cup heavy cream · 24 saffron threads · 1 orange
Green olives, minced, for garnish · Mixed sprouts, for garnish · Salt, to taste

1. In a large saucepan over medium heat, cook the codfish, milk, shallot, and bay leaves together for 20 minutes.
2. Discard the bay leaves and transfer the mixture to the bowl of a stand mixer fitted with the paddle attachment. Add the anchovies and beat the mixture on medium speed for 3 minutes, or until creamy. As the mixer is running, gradually add the oil until the mixture is whipped. Season with salt and set aside.
3. To a mixing bowl, add the Aperol, sugar, agar, and ½ cup of water and stir until well combined. Spread the mixture on a baking sheet lined with parchment paper into a 1⁄16-inch-thick layer. Set aside until gelled.
4. In the bowl of a stand mixer fitted with the paddle attachment, add the ricotta, chives, cream, and saffron and beat until creamy. Season with salt and set aside.
5. Peel and juice the orange and julienne the rind. In a small saucepan over low heat, combine the orange rind and juice and cook for 20–30 minutes, or until all the juice is cooked off.
6. Cut the gelatin layer into four 3½-by-5-inch rectangles. Spread equal portions of the creamed codfish onto the rectangles and roll them, forming cannoli.
7. Pour equal portions of the ricotta cream onto four serving plates. Place a cannolo on each of them, garnish with the minced olives, mixed sprouts, and cooked orange peel, and serve.

Recipe by Dario Parascandolo, executive chef, Restaurant Terrazza Danieli, Hotel Danieli

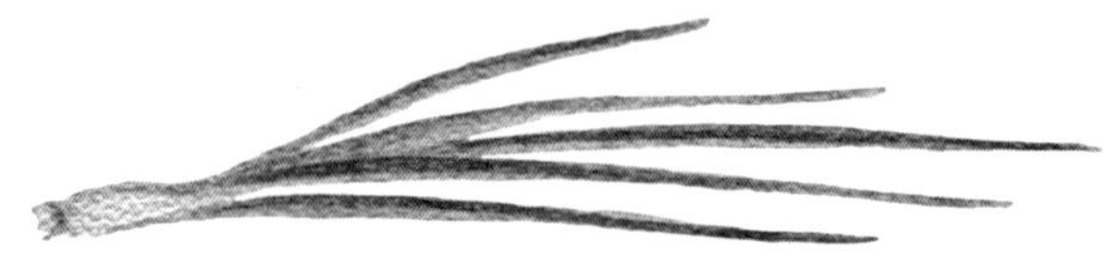

HOTEL DES INDES
THE HAGUE, NETHERLANDS

LANGOUSTINES À LA PLANCHA WITH BERGAMOT AND DAIKON

SERVES 4

3/8 cup plus 2 tsp olive oil · Bergamot zest, to taste · 12 slices daikon radish
Freshly squeezed juice of 1/2 a lime · 2 drops Tabasco
3 Tbsp unsalted butter · 12 langoustines, peeled and deveined · Salt, to taste

1 In a measuring cup, combine the oil and the bergamot zest. Set aside for 15 minutes to allow the flavors to infuse.

2 In a small bowl, season the daikon with the lime juice, Tabasco, 1 Tbsp of the bergamot-infused oil (reserve the remaining oil for later use), and salt and set aside.

3 Warm the butter on a plancha or other type of grill over high heat until browned. Place the langoustines in the butter and cook for 1 minute on each side.

4 To serve, place the langoustines on a plate and garnish with the daikon.

Recipe by Yke Cornelisse, sous chef, Hotel des Indes

HOTEL ELEPHANT
WEIMAR, GERMANY

RACK OF LAMB IN MEDITERRANEAN BREADED CRUST

SERVES 4

For the forcemeat (makes 4¼ oz):
4¼ oz raw turkey breast · ⅓ cup heavy cream · ½ tsp salt

For the glazed onions:
4 white onions, peeled and halved
¼ cup olive oil · ⅓ cup goat cheese (such as Caprino or Sainte-Maure, without ash)
1⅓ Tbsp panko (breadcrumbs) · 1 Tbsp chopped fresh chives
1 Tbsp unsalted butter, melted · Salt and freshly ground black pepper, to taste

For the racks of lamb:
4 (14½-oz) racks of lamb, bones Frenched and cleaned and silverskin removed
2 slices tramezzini (soft white) bread, diced
7 sun-dried tomatoes, diced · ¼ cup chopped pine nuts (pignolis)
1 sprig fresh rosemary, roughly chopped · 1 sprig fresh thyme, roughly chopped
4½ oz Forcemeat (above) · 4 cups peanut oil
Mashed potatoes, for serving · 1 recipe Glazed Onions (above), for serving
Salt and freshly ground black pepper, to taste

1 Make the forcemeat: In a blender, carefully process the turkey breast. Add the cream and blend again, then blend in the salt. The meat should be creamy but should not be warmed by the blending.

2 Make the glazed onions: Season the peeled onion halves with salt and pepper and drizzle the oil evenly on top. Place the onions on a microwavable plate, cover them with plastic wrap, and microwave on high for 5 minutes, or until completely softened (if they are not yet ready, cook for another 2 minutes and check; repeat if necessary). Set aside to cool.

3 Preheat the oven to 350°F. Line a baking sheet with parchment paper and place the onion halves, face up, on the baking sheet.

4 Remove 2–3 inner rings from each onion half and cut them into small pieces. In a mixing bowl, combine the chopped onion, goat cheese, panko, and chives and season with salt and pepper. Distribute the mixture over the onion halves. Pour the melted butter over the top and bake for 10–12 minutes, or until golden.

5 Make the racks of lamb: Place the racks of lamb in a vacuum-seal bags. Using a candy thermometer, bring a large pot of water over medium heat to 145°F. Add the sealed bags to the pot and cook for 35 minutes. Remove the lamb from the bags and pat dry. Season with salt and pepper.

6 In a wide, shallow mixing bowl, combine the bread, sun-dried tomatoes, pine nuts, rosemary, and thyme. Place the forcemeat in a separate wide, shallow mixing bowl.

7 Coat the racks of lamb with the forcemeat, then with the bread mixture.

8 Place a deep, heavy frying pan or Dutch oven over high heat. Add the oil and, using a candy thermometer, heat to over 350°F. Place the racks of lamb, one at a time, into the oil and deep-fry for 25–30 seconds, or until golden. Transfer them to a paper towel–lined plate for 5 minutes to drain, covered with foil to keep warm.

9 Serve with the mashed potatoes and glazed onions.

Recipe by Marcello Fabbri, executive chef, Restaurant Anna Amalia, Hotel Elephant

HOTEL FUERSTENHOF

LEIPZIG, GERMANY

MAGRET DUCK BREAST WITH PUMPKIN, ELDERBERRY-NUT VINAIGRETTE, AND SAUTÉED PORCINI MUSHROOMS

SERVES 4

For the pumpkin chips:
3¾ oz fresh Muscat pumpkin · ½ cup confectioners' sugar

For the elderberry-nut vinaigrette:
¼ cup elderberry vinegar · 3 Tbsp macadamia nut oil
3¾ oz fresh elderberries · Sea salt and freshly ground black pepper, to taste

For the nutmeg-pumpkin mash:
18 oz fresh Muscat pumpkin · ½ cup (1 stick) unsalted butter
1 tsp chopped fresh rosemary · 1 tsp chopped fresh thyme
1 pinch freshly grated nutmeg · Salt and freshly ground black pepper, to taste

For the duck breast:
4 (6½-oz) duck breasts, skin on · 1 Tbsp Maldon sea salt flakes
1 Tbsp Szechuan peppercorns · 2 tsp sunflower oil

For the porcini mushrooms:
1 Tbsp sunflower oil · 11 oz fresh porcini mushrooms
½ tsp minced fresh rosemary · ½ tsp minced fresh thyme
Salt and freshly ground black pepper, to taste

1 Make the pumpkin chips: Preheat the oven to 250°F. Peel the pumpkin, remove and discard the seeds, cut the flesh into thin slices, and place them on a baking sheet lined with parchment paper. Dust the slices with the sugar and bake for 20 minutes, or until crisp. Set aside to cool.

2 Make the elderberry-nut vinaigrette: In a small bowl, combine the vinegar and oil. Season with salt and pepper and whisk vigorously until well combined. Add the elderberries and set aside for 2 hours to marinate.

3 Make the nutmeg-pumpkin mash: Peel the pumpkin, remove and discard the seeds, and chop the flesh into small pieces.

4 In a saucepan over medium heat, combine the butter, rosemary, thyme, and nutmeg. Season with salt and pepper. Add the pumpkin pieces and cook for about 20 minutes, or until softened. Remove from the heat, set aside some of the pieces for finishing, then mash the remaining pieces with a masher. Press through a sieve and set aside.

5 Prepare the duck breasts: Preheat the oven to 275°F. Cut out the sinews of the duck breasts and cut the fat side crosswise. Season with the sea salt and peppercorns.

6 In an oven-safe pan over medium heat, warm the oil. Add the duck breasts, skin-side down, and sauté for 3 minutes, or until crispy. Place in the oven for 5 minutes, or until a thermometer inserted into the meat registers 127.4°F. Set aside for 5 minutes to rest.

7 Prepare the porcini mushrooms: In a sauté pan over high heat, warm the oil. Add the mushrooms, rosemary, and thyme and sauté for 2 minutes, or until browned. Remove from the heat and season with salt and pepper.

8 To serve, spoon the hot pumpkin mash onto four warmed serving plates. Carve the duck breasts and arrange equal portions on each plate next to the mash. Arrange the sautéed mushrooms around the plates. Pour the vinaigrette over the duck, add the pumpkin chips and reserved pumpkin pieces, and serve.

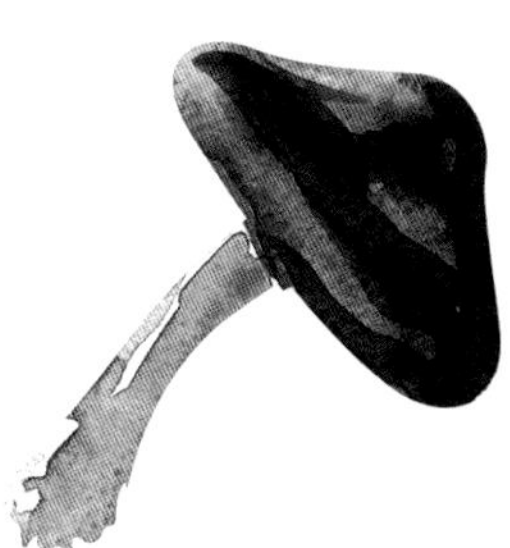

HOTEL GOLDENER HIRSCH
SALZBURG, AUSTRIA

TAFELSPITZ (PRIME BOILED BEEF)

SERVES 6-8

1 onion, with skin on, halved · 4 1/3 lb beef tenderloin
2 oz carrots, cubed, plus more, julienned, for garnish · 2 oz yellow carrots, cubed
2 oz celery stalks, cubed · 2 oz parsley root, chopped, plus more, julienned, for garnish
1/2 leek, chopped · 5–10 black peppercorns · Beef bouillon powder, to taste (optional)
1/2 cup chopped fresh chives, for garnish · Salt, to taste

1 In a dry pan, heat the onion halves on the cut side until the cut surface becomes dark brown. Remove from the heat.

2 In a large pot, bring 2⅔ quarts of water to a boil. Add the beef, reduce the heat to low, and cook for 10–15 minutes, regularly skimming off any debris. Add the onion halves, mixed vegetables, and peppercorns and simmer on low heat (just below the boiling point) for 2–2½ hours, continuing to skim the surface regularly. Add the bouillon powder, if using. Remove from the heat.

3 Remove the beef from the broth and cut it into finger-thick slices. Arrange in a serving bowl, season with salt, and garnish with the chives. Strain and reserve the broth and season with salt. Discard the vegetables. Pour the broth over the beef slices, garnish with the julienned vegetables, and serve.

HOTEL GRANDE BRETAGNE
ATHENS, GREECE

KRITHAROTO WITH SHRIMP

SERVES 4

½ cup olive oil · 1 onion, finely chopped · 2 scallions, white portion only, finely chopped
1 clove garlic, crushed · 12 oz orzo pasta · ¼ cup white wine
2 tomatoes, peeled and chopped · 1 sprig basil, finely chopped · 1 bay leaf
1½ quarts fish broth · 16 Symi shrimp, peeled and deveined
1½ cups grated Gruyère cheese · 2 Tbsp unsalted butter
Salt and freshly ground black pepper, to taste

1 In a large saucepan over medium heat, warm the oil. Add the onion, scallions, and garlic and sauté for 3–4 minutes. Add the orzo and stir; add the wine. Cook for 1–2 minutes, or until the wine has been absorbed.

2 Add the tomatoes, basil, and bay leaf to the saucepan and season with salt and pepper. Gradually add the fish broth to the saucepan and cook, stirring constantly, for about 17 minutes, or until all the broth has been absorbed. About 2–3 minutes before removing from the heat, add the shrimp.

3 Remove from the heat and add the Gruyère and butter. Stir well until fully blended; discard the bay leaf.

4 Transfer to a hot platter and serve.

HOTEL IMPERIAL
VIENNA, AUSTRIA

MARINATED SALMON TROUT WITH CUCUMBERS, SUNFLOWER SEEDS, AND ROSE BLOSSOM GRANITA

SERVES 4

For the cucumbers:
4 1/2 lb whole lemon cucumbers · Fresh dill, chopped, to taste
3/4 cup plus 2 Tbsp chardonnay wine vinegar · 1/3 cup granulated sugar · 1 Tbsp salt · 2 bay leaves
1 dash white peppercorns · 1 dash mustard seed · 1 tsp freshly squeezed lemon juice
1 tsp sunflower oil · Salt and freshly ground black pepper, to taste

For the salmon trout:
1 (8 1/2 oz) whole salmon trout fillet, deboned · 1/2 cup gin · 1/3 cup sea salt
1/2 bunch fresh dill · Freshly squeezed juice and finely grated zest of 1/2 an orange
Freshly squeezed juice and finely grated zest of 1/2 a lemon
2 Tbsp plus 2 tsp roasted sunflower seeds, for serving · Fresh herbs, for garnish

For the rose blossom granita:
2 tsp freshly grated ginger · Freshly squeezed lemon juice, to taste
1 pinch granulated sugar · 1/4 cup gin · 1/2 Tbsp dried rose blossoms · 1/4 cup crème fraîche
1 tsp red beet juice · Salt and freshly ground black pepper, to taste

1 Prepare the cucumbers: In sterile canning jars, layer the cucumbers and dill.

2 In a large saucepan over high heat, bring 2 cups of water to a boil. Add the vinegar, sugar, 1 Tbsp of salt, bay leaves, peppercorns, and mustard seed and allow to simmer for 3 minutes. Remove from the heat. Pour the hot mixture evenly over the cucumbers in the jars. Seal the jars and immediately turn them upside down. Set aside for at least 1 week to marinate.

3 Remove the cucumbers from the jars and discard the juice and bay leaves. Thinly slice the cucumbers lengthwise and place them in a container with the lemon juice and oil. Season with salt and pepper.

4 Prepare the salmon trout: In a shallow dish, combine all the ingredients except the sunflower seeds and fresh herbs. Refrigerate for 12 hours to marinate. Remove the fish from the marinade, rinse with water, and slice into four fillets.

5 Make the granita: In a small saucepan over high heat, combine the ginger, lemon juice, sugar, and 1 cup plus 1 Tbsp of water. Season with salt and pepper and bring to a boil. Add the gin and rose blossoms and remove from the heat. Set aside for 20 minutes to infuse.

6 Strain the infusion into a metal bowl; discard the solids. Add the crème fraîche and beet juice and mix until well combined. Freeze for 1 hour, removing every 10 minutes to scrape with a fork, making small ice crystals.

7 To serve, warm the fillets in a 175°F oven for 4 minutes. Transfer to a serving platter and sprinkle with the roasted sunflower seeds. Arrange the marinated cucumber slices next to the fillets. Garnish with the fresh herbs. Sprinkle the cucumbers with the rose blossom granita and serve.

HOTEL MARIA CRISTINA
SAN SEBASTIÁN, SPAIN

JIM-LET FOX-TROT

SERVES 1

2 oz Bombay Original gin · 1 oz Rose's lime juice
1 bottle Original Indian Schweppes tonic water · Lime zest

1 In a cocktail shaker filled with ice, combine the gin and lime juice. Stir for about 15 seconds and pour into a chilled glass. Wrap the ice in a cloth and hit it against a hard surface to make slush. Pour the slush into the chilled glass, making an iced gimlet.

2 In a tall glass, place 7 ice cubes and the tonic water. Add ¼ cup plus 2 Tbsp of the iced gimlet, garnish with lime zest, and serve.

"This is the most genuine representative of the dry tonics, and my homage to the exalted Gin & Tonic."

JAVIER DE LAS MUELAS
mixologist, Hotel Maria Cristina

JAVIER DE LAS MUELAS

mixologist, Hotel Maria Cristina, San Sebastián, Spain

YOUR FAVORITE INGREDIENT TO USE WHEN PREPARING A COCKTAIL?

Droplets are a product of our creation that I never get tired of experimenting with. They are drops of the essence of twelve flavors, one hundred percent natural and without alcohol. I am proud to think that they are my contribution to the world of bar culture.

IN WHICH RECIPES DOES THIS INGREDIENT WORK BEST?

The diversity of flavors, ranging from rosemary to Indian spices, from violets to freshly cut celery, give great versatility and allow use in alcoholic and nonalcoholic cocktails.

YOUR FAVORITE COCKTAIL TO PREPARE?

A dry martini, for its simplicity—and then its complexity. It is a magical communion of ingredients where no error can be masked. For me, it is interpreting a lifestyle.

WHAT IS A COCKTAIL NO ONE SHOULD VISIT SAN SEBASTIÁN WITHOUT DRINKING?

I recommend one of our classics that cannot be missed: the Jim-Let Fox-Trot. A delicious homage to the exalted gin and tonic, which consists of a gimlet granita (a classic cocktail made with Bombay Sapphire and Rose's lime juice), which we serve floating over Schweppes Premium Mixer tonic.

YOUR PREFERRED COMFORT FOOD AND DRINK?

Hake kokotxas pil-pil and grilled turbot or squid, all preceded by a frosted, very dry martini and washed down with a very fresh Txakoli (sparkling, dry white wine).

HOTEL MARQUES DE RISCAL
ELCIEGO, SPAIN

RED WINE CAVIAR OVER FOIE GRAS

SERVES 10

For the red wine reduction:
1½ cups red wine · ¼ cup granulated sugar
¾ tsp agar · 1 cup plus 1 Tbsp sunflower oil

For the foie gras:
4 oz foie gras, cleaned and veins removed · 2 sheets gelatin
3 Tbsp heavy cream · ½ tsp red wine · 1 dash salt · ½ dash white pepper

For serving:
1 (1½-oz) tin caviar

1 Make the red wine reduction: In a medium saucepan over medium heat, combine the wine and sugar with ½ cup plus 1 Tbsp of water and bring to a boil. Add the agar and boil for 2 minutes. Remove from the heat.

2 Place the oil in a metal bowl partially submerged in a bowl filled with ice water. Fill a syringe with the wine-and-sugar mixture and let it trickle into the oil. Set aside.

3 Prepare the foie gras: Bring a saucepan of water to a boil. Drop the foie gras into the boiling water and scald for 1 minute. Remove from the heat, then remove the foie gras from the hot water. Soften the gelatin sheets by placing them in a bowl of cold water. When softened, remove the gelatin, squeeze out the excess water, and set aside.

4 In a small saucepan over medium-low heat, combine the foie gras, cream, and red wine with 2 Tbsp of water. Using a thermometer, bring the contents of the saucepan to 150°F. While maintaining that steady temperature, use an immersion blender to blend the mixture until it is smooth and even.

5 Transfer the mixture to a bowl. Add the red wine reduction, gelatin, salt, and pepper to the bowl and stir until well combined.

6 To serve, spoon the contents of the caviar tin into a small bowl and transfer the foie gras mixture to the empty tin. Top the foie gras with the caviar and serve.

HOTEL NATIONAL
MOSCOW, RUSSIA

SMOKED SALMON SALAD

SERVES 4

For the salmon salad:
2 cups mixed salad greens, washed and patted dry · 5 oz smoked salmon, sliced
4 oz cherry tomatoes, halved · 3 oz cucumber, thinly sliced · 4 tsp minced shallot
4 quail eggs, boiled and halved, for garnish · 2 oz Kalamata olives, for garnish
1 oz radishes, sliced, for garnish · 2 tsp minced fresh dill, for garnish
1 tsp red caviar, for garnish

For the vinaigrette:
2 Tbsp plus 2 tsp olive oil · 2 Tbsp plus 2 tsp freshly squeezed lemon juice
2 tsp capers · 2 tsp Dijon mustard · Salt and freshly ground black pepper, to taste

1 Make the salmon salad: Arrange equal portions of the salad greens in the center of four serving plates. Add equal portions of the smoked salmon, tomatoes, cucumber, and shallot.

2 Make the vinaigrette: In a mixing bowl, combine the oil, lemon juice, capers, and mustard and whisk until very well combined. Season with salt and pepper.

3 To serve, drizzle the vinaigrette over each salmon salad and garnish each with a quail egg and equal portions of the olives, radishes, dill, and caviar.

Recipe by Anatoly Kharchenko, executive chef, Hotel National

HOTEL PITRIZZA
PORTO CERVO, ITALY

PAN-SEARED OCTOPUS WITH CRISPY VEGETABLE SALAD

SERVES 4

2 cups songino (lamb's lettuce) greens · 2 cups mixed salad greens
2 cups chicory greens · 1 cup finely grated carrots · 1 bulb fennel, chopped
5 Tbsp olive oil, divided · 1 cup freshly squeezed lemon juice
4 small (1⅓–1½-lb) fresh octopuses, tentacles only, cut into cubes
2 Tbsp sun-dried tomatoes · 1 Tbsp finely chopped fresh parsley
1 Tbsp finely chopped fresh basil · Salt and freshly ground black pepper, to taste

1 In a large serving bowl, combine the songino, mixed salad, and chicory greens. Add the carrots and fennel and toss until well combined. Drizzle with the lemon juice and 1 Tbsp of the oil and season with salt.

2 In a sauté pan over medium-high heat, warm 1 Tbsp of the oil. Add one-fourth of the octopus cubes, season with salt and pepper, and sear for 2–3 minutes on each side. Transfer the sautéed cubes to a plate and cover them with foil.

3 Repeat until all the octopus has been sautéed, adding 1 Tbsp of the oil with each batch. Remove the pan from the heat, add the sun-dried tomatoes, parsley, and basil, and stir until well combined.

4 Transfer the contents of the pan to the bowl containing the greens. Serve the octopus over the salad.

Recipe by Franco Guardone, executive chef, Hotel Pitrizza

HOTEL PRESIDENT WILSON
GENEVA, SWITZERLAND

CHOCOLATE SOUFFLÉ TARTS

SERVES 10

For the crust:
1/2 cup (1 stick) unsalted butter, cubed and very cold
1 1/2 cups plus 2 Tbsp all-purpose flour · 1/2 cup granulated sugar
1 large egg, beaten · 1 pinch salt

For the ganache:
9 oz bittersweet chocolate (preferably Guanaja 70%), chopped · 1 large egg
1 cup plus 1 Tbsp heavy whipping cream · 3/8 cup plus 1 Tbsp whole milk

For the chocolate soufflé:
2 large eggs · 5 large egg yolks · 5 1/2 Tbsp superfine sugar
4 1/2 oz bittersweet chocolate (preferably Guanaja 70%), chopped
1/2 cup light cream · 2 Tbsp all-purpose flour
Double crème de la Gruyère (a very rich double cream), for serving

1 Make the crust: Preheat the oven to 350°F. Line a baking sheet with parchment paper.

2 In a mixing bowl, cut the cold butter into the flour using a fork or pastry cutter. Add the sugar, egg, and salt and stir until well combined.

3 Dust a clean work surface with flour and turn out the dough onto the surface. Sprinkle a little more flour on top of the dough and roll it out to a 1½-inch thickness. Cut out ten 2¾-inch circles and place them on the prepared baking sheet.

4 Bake for 8–12 minutes. Remove from the oven and set aside to cool to room temperature.

5 Make the ganache: Preheat the oven to 375°F. Line a baking sheet with parchment paper.

6 Place the chocolate and the egg in a medium heatproof mixing bowl.

7 Place the cream and milk in a small saucepan over medium-high heat. Bring just to a boil.

8 Very gradually (only ⅓ cup at a time) pour the hot cream mixture over the chocolate and egg, stirring to thoroughly combine after each addition.

9 Pour the ganache onto the baking sheet, spread it out evenly, and bake for 5 minutes. Remove from the oven and transfer the baked ganache to the refrigerator to cool completely.

10 Once the ganache is fully chilled, cut it into ten 2¾-inch circles.

11 Make the soufflé: Make a zabaglione using the double-boiler technique—Place 1 inch of water in a saucepan over high heat and bring to a boil. Place a medium heatproof mixing bowl on top of the saucepan, making sure the bowl does not touch the water. Add the whole eggs, egg yolks, and sugar to the bowl. Using an electric hand mixer set on the highest speed, beat the eggs and sugar together for 4–5 minutes, or until the mixture is thick and the sugar has completely dissolved. Remove from the heat.

12 Make a second ganache: Place the chocolate in a medium heatproof mixing bowl.

13 Place the cream in a small saucepan over medium-high heat. Bring just to a boil.

14 Pour the hot cream over the chocolate. Add the flour and whisk vigorously until the mixture is smooth and all the chocolate has melted.

15 Mix the zabaglione and ganache with a silicone spatula until well combined. Divide the mixture evenly into a silicone mold with 10 circle cavities measuring 2¾-inches in diameter. Freeze for at least 60 minutes.

16 Preheat the oven to 400°F. Line a baking sheet with parchment paper.

17 Place each frozen soufflé on each crust circle on the prepared baking sheet and bake for 5–6 minutes. Remove from the oven.

18 To serve, set one ganache circle on each serving plate and place 1 baked soufflé tart on top. Serve with the double crème de la Gruyère.

Recipe by Didier Steudler, pastry chef, Hotel President Wilson

HOTEL ROMAZZINO
PORTO CERVO, ITALY

PASTA SALAD WITH LOBSTER, PACHINO TOMATOES, TAGGIASCA OLIVES, AVOCADO, AND BUFFALO MOZZARELLA

SERVES 4

1 lb Pachino tomatoes · Dark brown sugar, to taste · 1 (1–1⅛-lb) whole live lobster
11½ oz Khorasan wheat fusilli pasta · 3¾ oz Taggiasca olives
3¾ oz buffalo mozzarella, sliced · 1 avocado, diced
Fresh green and red basil, sliced, for garnish
Wild fennel, chopped, for garnish · Extra-virgin olive oil, for drizzling
Salt and freshly ground black pepper, to taste

1. Prepare the tomatoes: Preheat the oven to 200°F. Line a baking sheet with parchment paper. Cut the tomatoes in half and place them on the baking sheet. Sprinkle with the brown sugar and season with salt and pepper. Bake for 2 hours. Remove from the oven and set aside to cool.
2. Prepare the lobster: Fill a large pot with 1 inch of water; bring to a boil and salt generously. Add the lobster, cover, and cook until bright red, 8–10 minutes.
3. Transfer the lobster to a rimmed baking sheet and let cool. Crack the lobster shell, pick the meat from the tail and claws, cut the meat into ½-inch pieces, and set aside. Discard the shell.
4. Cook the pasta according to the package directions to al dente.
5. Transfer the pasta to a serving bowl and toss with the tomatoes, lobster, and olives. Top with the mozzarella and avocado. Garnish with the basil and fennel, drizzle the oil over the top, and serve.

Recipe by Giovanni Oggiana, executive chef, Hotel Romazzino

KING GEORGE
ATHENS, GREECE

AEGEAN FISH SOUP

SERVES 4

For the aioli:
2 cloves garlic, peeled and minced · 1 large egg yolk · 1/2 cup plus 1 Tbsp olive oil
1 Tbsp freshly squeezed lemon juice · 1 Tbsp white vinegar
4 slices toasted bread, for serving · Fine salt and freshly ground black pepper, to taste

For the soup:
1 1/8 lb grouper · 1 1/8 lb scorpionfish · 2 onions (1 quartered and 1 peeled and chopped)
2 stalks celery, chopped, divided · 3 carrots, chopped, divided
1/2 cup plus 1 Tbsp olive oil · 1 clove garlic, peeled and minced
1/2 lb fennel bulb, chopped · 1 russet potato, cubed · 1 leek, white part only, chopped
1/4 cup white wine vinegar · 1 tomato, seeded and chopped · 1/2 tsp fennel seed
1 star anise · 5–6 saffron threads · 1/4 cup fresh cilantro · 1/4 cup fresh thyme
1/4 cup fresh Greek parsley · Freshly squeezed juice of 1 lemon
12 fresh mussels · 12 fresh shrimp, 3–4 inches each
Fine salt and freshly ground black pepper, to taste

1 Make the aioli: In a mixing bowl, mash the garlic and season with salt and pepper. Add the egg yolk. While whisking constantly, gradually add the oil. Once one-fourth of the oil has been blended in, add the remaining oil in larger amounts until thickened. Whisk in the lemon juice and vinegar.

2 Make the soup: Clean and fillet the fish and refrigerate until ready for use. Place the bones and 3 quarts of water in a large pot over high heat and bring to a boil. Add the quartered onion, half of the celery, and one-third of the carrots. Continue boiling for 30 minutes, occasionally skimming off any debris. Strain, discarding the solids, and set aside.

3 In a large pot over high heat, warm the oil. Add the garlic and cook for 3–4 minutes, or until golden. Add all the remaining vegetables and sauté for 4–5 minutes. Add the vinegar and deglaze the pot. Add the broth, fennel seed, and star anise and bring to a boil, occasionally skimming off any debris. Reduce the heat to medium, add the saffron, herbs, and lemon juice, and simmer for 30 minutes. Transfer to a blender and blend until smooth. Strain into a serving bowl and season with salt and pepper; cover with foil to keep warm.

4 Steam the fish and seafood: In a large lidded pot fitted with a steamer insert, bring 1 inch of water to a boil. Place the fillets, mussels, and shrimp in the steamer insert, cover, and steam for 4–5 minutes. Remove from the heat.

5 To serve, transfer the fish and seafood to hot serving plates. Serve with the hot soup, aioli, and toasted bread.

LUGAL

ANKARA, TURKEY

THE ANISETTE

SERVES 1

1 1/3 oz Raki (an unsweetened anise-flavored aperitif)
1 1/3 oz cranberry liqueur · 2/3 oz Baileys Irish Cream liqueur
Grated chocolate, for rimming · 5 coffee beans, for garnish
1 star anise, for garnish · 1 strawberry, for garnish

1 In a cocktail shaker filled with ice, combine the liquid ingredients. Shake and strain into a martini glass rimmed with the grated chocolate.

2 Place the coffee beans and star anise on top, garnish with the strawberry, and serve.

METROPOL PALACE
BELGRADE, SERBIA

GRILLED GOAT CHEESE WITH BEET FOAM

SERVES 4

For the beet foam:
10 oz (about 3 small) beetroots, peeled · 1/4 cup loosely packed dark brown sugar
3/4 cup sour cream · 1/2 cup celery root, peeled and diced · 1/2 Tbsp lecithin (optional)

For the goat cheese:
3 1/2 Tbsp olive oil · 1 3/4 Tbsp ground white pepper
1 lb Serbian goat cheese, cut into 3/8-inch-wide pieces

For the pine puts:
2 Tbsp salted butter · 1 1/4 oz pine nuts (pignolis) · 1 Tbsp chopped fresh rosemary

For serving:
2 cups wild arugula, chilled in ice · Extra-virgin olive oil, for drizzling

1 Prepare the beets: Preheat the oven to 350°F. Line a baking sheet with parchment paper. Place the beets on the prepared baking sheet and bake for 35 minutes, or until they are softened and releasing their juice. Remove the beets from the oven; roll them in the brown sugar until well coated.

2 Transfer the beets to a skillet over medium heat and cook for 12 minutes, or until caramelized. Add the sour cream and celery root to the skillet and cook for another 15 minutes, or until completely soft.

3 Make the beet foam: Transfer the contents of the skillet to a blender and process for 3 minutes, or until completely creamy. Combine the contents of the blender and the lecithin in a saucepan over medium heat and bring to a boil. The top will foam; skim the foam off for use in the dish.

4 Prepare the goat cheese: In a wide, shallow dish, combine the oil and black pepper and roll the pieces of goat cheese in the mixture. Transfer the coated pieces of cheese to a pan over medium heat and cook for 3 minutes on each side, or until the crust is crispy and the interior is soft. Remove from the heat.

5 Prepare the pine nuts: In a frying pan over medium heat, warm the butter. Add the pine nuts and rosemary and fry for 2–4 minutes, or until golden. Remove from the heat.

6 To serve, spread equal amounts of the beet foam on four serving plates. Arrange equal portions of the chilled arugula over the foam and place equal portions of the goat cheese slices on it. Top each with the nuts and rosemary and a drizzle of olive oil and serve.

Recipe by Dimitrije Acevski, executive Chef, Metropol Palace

MYSTIQUE

SANTORINI, GREECE

AMBERJACK CEVICHE IN LIME JUICE WITH GINGER AND FLORINA PEPPERS

SERVES 4

1 roasted red Florina pepper, finely chopped · 1 tsp peeled and chopped fresh ginger
$^{1}/_{2}$ tsp honey · Freshly squeezed juice of $^{1}/_{2}$ a lime · $^{1}/_{4}$ cup plus 1 Tbsp extra-virgin olive oil
$1^{1}/_{4}$ lb amberjack (or other lean white fish) fillet, cut into bite-size pieces
1 Tbsp chopped fresh chives · 4 cherry tomatoes, quartered, for garnish
Salt and freshly ground black pepper, to taste

1. In a large mixing bowl, combine the pepper, ginger, honey, and lime juice. While whisking gently and constantly, gradually add the oil until the mixture becomes uniform and creamy.
2. Add the fish and then the chives to the bowl and season with salt and pepper. Set aside for 5 minutes to marinate.
3. Transfer the ceviche to four serving plates and garnish each serving with a tomato. Sprinkle the marinade over the serving plates and serve.

Recipe by Melina Chomata, executive chef, Mystique

THE PARK TOWER KNIGHTSBRIDGE

LONDON, GREAT BRITAIN

THE HAZE TOWER

SERVES 1

For the rosemary-infused honey (makes 2¼ cups):
1 cup honey · 1 cup hot water · 10 sprigs rosemary

For the Earl Grey and English Breakfast tea infusion:
1 tea bag or 1 tsp loose-leaf Earl Grey tea
1 tea bag or 1 tsp loose-leaf English Breakfast tea · ⅓ cup hot water

For the Haze Tower:
1¼ oz Octomore whiskey · 1 oz Earl Grey and English Breakfast Tea Infusion (above)
½ oz egg white · 1 Tbsp Rosemary-Infused Honey (above)
2 tsp freshly squeezed lemon juice · 2–3 drops orange bitters
Dried orange wheel, for garnish · 1 sprig rosemary, for garnish

1 Make the rosemary-infused honey: Dilute the honey with the hot water and stir until blended. Add the rosemary and pour into a sealed jar. Refrigerate for 2–3 days to infuse. (The syrup will keep in the refrigerator for up to 3 months.)

2 Make the Earl Grey and English Breakfast tea infusion: Infuse the teas together in the hot water for 4 minutes.

3 Make the cocktail: To a cocktail shaker filled with ice, add the whiskey, tea infusion, egg white, rosemary-infused honey, lemon juice, and orange bitters. Shake until well blended.

4 Pour over ice into a highball glass. Garnish with the dried orange wheel and rosemary sprig and serve.

PINE CLIFFS
ALGARVE, PORTUGAL

CATAPLANA OF FISH AND SEAFOOD

SERVES 4

11 oz stone bass fillet, skin on · 11 oz monkfish loin, cleaned
8 small young potatoes, washed, peeled, and halved
2 onions, peeled and julienned · 2 very ripe tomatoes, washed and cut into wheels
1 green bell pepper, julienned · 1 red bell pepper, julienned
4 cloves garlic, peeled and thinly sliced, divided · 1 Tbsp chopped fresh cilantro
1 Tbsp chopped fresh river mint · 1 small fresh chili pepper, julienned
1 bay leaf · 6½ Tbsp olive oil · 6½ Tbsp white wine
11 oz (13–15) medium shrimp, heads on · 7¼ oz clams from the Ria Formosa
Sea salt flakes from the Ria Formosa, to taste

1 Cut the bass and monkfish into generous chunks and season with sea salt.

2 In a cataplana or conventional steamer pot over low heat, combine the potatoes, onions, tomatoes, bell peppers, and garlic. Season with sea salt. Add the bass, monkfish, chili pepper, bay leaf, and half of the cilantro and river mint. Add the oil and wine and top with the shrimp and the clams. Close the cataplana and cook for 10 minutes, or 4 minutes if using a steamer pot. Raise the heat to high and cook for 1 more minute. Discard the bay leaf.

3 Transfer to a platter, garnish with the remaining cilantro and river mint, and serve immediately.

Recipe by Marco Alban, executive chef, Pine Cliffs

PRINCE DE GALLES

PARIS, FRANCE

LUKEWARM SLIGHTLY TART EGG YOLKS, ASPARAGUS, CREAMED MORELS, AND BUCKWHEAT CIRCLES

SERVES 6

For the asparagus siphon:

1 Tbsp olive oil

2 lb 3 oz fresh asparagus, rough ends removed, peeled and finely chopped

1 onion, finely chopped · 1/2 tsp salt · 2/3 cup chicken broth · 1 tsp agar

For the asparagus mash:

3/8 cup chicken broth · 2 Tbsp olive oil · 2 cloves garlic · 1 1/3 tsp salt

1 1/8 lb green asparagus, rough ends trimmed, peeled and cut into 1/8-inch pieces

3 Tbsp freshly squeezed lemon juice · Finely grated zest of 1 lemon

Salt and freshly ground black pepper, to taste

For the egg yolks:

2 cups chicken broth · 2/3 cup sherry wine vinegar · 6 large egg yolks

For the buckwheat circles:

3 buckwheat crepes, prepared using a ready-made buckwheat crepe or pancake mix

For the creamed morels:

1/2 cup olive oil · 2 shallots, peeled and finely chopped

1 lb 1 oz fresh morel mushrooms, well cleaned and stalks removed and discarded

3/4 cup chicken broth · 2 Tbsp unsalted butter · 3 Tbsp veal stock

1 1/4 cups heavy cream · 2 Tbsp vin jaune (a French wine similar to dry fino sherry)

For serving:

6 asparagus tips, very thinly sliced · 2 tsp olive oil, for coating

3 Tbsp veal stock · 4 tsp sherry wine vinegar

1 oz small fresh morel mushrooms, well cleaned and stalks removed and discarded

2 scallions, sliced diagonally · 3 Tbsp unpasteurized heavy cream

3/4 oz wild garlic (Allium ericetorum) leaves

Fleur de sel and freshly ground black pepper, to taste

1. Make the asparagus siphon: In a skillet over medium heat, warm the oil. Add the asparagus, onion, and salt and fry for 5 minutes, or until the onion is translucent. Add the broth and ½ cup of water, bring to a simmer, and cook for 8 minutes, or until the vegetables are well blanched.
2. Transfer the contents of the skillet to a powerful blender and puree; strain the contents of the blender through a muslin chinois or fine-mesh sieve into a bowl.

continued on following page

continued from previous page

3 Transfer one-fourth of the contents of the bowl to a small pan over medium heat. Add the agar and simmer for 3 minutes, stirring constantly. Transfer the contents of the bowl and the pan into a cream whipper charged with carbon dioxide.

4 Make the asparagus mash: In a large pot over high heat, combine the broth, oil, garlic, and the 1⅓ tsp of salt. Add the asparagus and cook for 8 minutes. Drain through a colander and set aside to cool completely.

5 Once cooled, discard the garlic and transfer the asparagus to a bowl. Using a fork, mash the asparagus. Add the lemon juice and zest, then season with salt and pepper. Set aside.

6 Prepare the egg yolks: In a medium saucepan over medium heat, warm the chicken broth and sherry vinegar. Once the mixture is lukewarm, gently add the egg yolks, then remove from the heat. Set aside for 10 minutes to marinate.

7 Make the buckwheat circles: Prepare the crepes according to the package directions.

8 Preheat the oven to 350°F.

9 Cut four ½-inch-wide disks out of the crepes. In the center of each disk, cut out another 1¼-inch disk. Place the larger disks between two baking sheets and dry them in the oven for 8 minutes. Remove from the oven.

10 Make the morels: In a sauté pan over high heat, warm the oil. Add the shallots and cook for about 5 minutes, or until slightly browned. Add the morels and cook for 3 minutes, or until they release their water. Add the chicken broth and cook for 5 minutes. Remove from the heat and set aside.

11 When ready to serve, in a sauté pan over medium heat, warm the butter until foamy. Add the sautéed morel mixture and cook for 3 minutes. Deglaze the pan with the veal stock and add the cream and vin jaune. Cook for 5 minutes to bind the sauce.

12 To serve, coat the asparagus slices with the oil. In a small bowl, combine the veal stock and the sherry vinegar and set aside.

13 Garnish each of the smaller buckwheat disks with the small morels, the scallions, a dash of the raw cream, the wild garlic leaves, and the asparagus slices.

14 Place the asparagus mash in the center of a serving platter and arrange the creamed morels around it. Dispense the asparagus from the siphon in the center, on top of the mash. Top the asparagus with the marinated egg yolks and veal stock–sherry vinegar mixture and season with the fleur de sel and pepper. Place the larger, dried buckwheat disks over the dish in such a way that only the egg yolks are visible and serve.

Recipe by Stephanie Le Quellec, executive chef, Prince de Galles

ELISABETH VON THURN UND TAXIS

journalist

YOUR FAVORITE LOCAL PLACE TO EAT?

Market on avenue Matignon—not very French, but so yummy!

YOUR BEST MEAL THERE?

The crispy sushi and the shrimp and avocado salad.

FAVORITE INGREDIENT IN A DISH?

A good sea salt and great-quality olive oil.

YOUR FAVORITE FOOD AND DRINK PAIRING?

A strong black cup of coffee and dark chocolate.

THE BEST QUALITY ABOUT THE LOCAL CUISINE?

France has pristine produce and takes pride in its preparation.

WHAT DISH REMINDS YOU OF HOME?

A perfect breakfast. Germans love their breakfast, and I adore a good, grainy whole-grain bread.

YOUR PREFERRED COMFORT FOOD?

Generally anything home-prepared and eaten with friends. A good gnocchi alla siciliana can make anyone happy!

THE ROMANOS
COSTA NAVARINO, GREECE

OLIVE OIL MARTINI

SERVES 1

For the olive oil syrup:
3¼ cups olive oil · 30 basil leaves · 20 baby arugula leaves
20 cilantro leaves · 5 sprigs rosemary · 5 sprigs oregano

For the clarified lemon juice:
7 cups lemon juice · 1 tsp agar

For the Olive Oil Martini:
1¾ oz dry gin · 2½ Tbsp Clarified Lemon Juice (above) · 1½ Tbsp Olive Oil Syrup (above)
2 tsp Mastiha liqueur (a liqueur seasoned with mastic) · 2 tsp pear liqueur
10 drops extra-virgin olive oil

1 Make the olive oil syrup: In a jar with a tight-fitting lid, combine all the ingredients and set aside in a cool, dark place for 2 days to infuse.

2 Using cheesecloth, double-strain the infused oil into a bottle with a tight seal.

3 Make the clarified lemon juice: Finely strain the lemon juice into a stainless-steel bowl. Dip the stainless bowl into a bowl of ice water, ensuring that none of the water enters the stainless bowl.

4 In a saucepan over medium-high heat, combine the agar with 1¼ cups of water and bring to a boil. Simmer for 1 minute, then whisk the agar mixture into the lemon juice and set aside for 10 minutes.

5 Using a large strainer covered with a cloth, strain the lemon juice mixture. For purer juice, repeat the process through a coffee filter.

6 Make the cocktail: In a cocktail shaker filled with ice, combine all the ingredients except the extra-virgin olive oil and shake well. Double-strain into a martini glass and add the drops of extra-virgin olive oil.

Recipe by Aristotelis Papadopoulos, mixologist, Anax Lounge, The Romanos

SANTA MARINA
MYKONOS, GREECE

STEAMED PRAWNS WITH SAFFRON AND LIME

SERVES 4

8 king prawns · 2 Tbsp extra-virgin olive oil · 1 cup plus 1 Tbsp fish stock
3–4 saffron threads · 1 Tbsp Noilly Prat vermouth · 2 tsp white wine
1 shallot, peeled and minced · 2 tomatoes, seeded and diced
Freshly squeezed juice of 1/4 lime · Lime wedges, for garnish
Salt and freshly ground black pepper, to taste

1. Remove the shells from the prawns, except from the last section of the tail. Devein, wash, and pat dry. Rub with the oil and set aside for 30 minutes.
2. In a small saucepan over high heat, warm the fish stock. Add the saffron and cook for 3 minutes, or until the saffron infuses the stock.
3. In a large lidded saucepan over medium heat, combine the vermouth, white wine, and shallot and cook for 3–4 minutes, or until the volume is reduced by half. Add the warmed fish stock infusion and cook for 10 minutes, or until the volume is reduced again by half. Strain the sauce through a sieve and return to the saucepan.
4. Add the tomatoes and simmer for 3 minutes. Season with salt and pepper and add the lime juice. Remove from the heat and cover to keep warm.
5. Prepare the prawns: Season the prawns with salt and pepper.
6. Fill a pot with 1 inch of water; bring to a boil and salt generously. Add the prawns, cover, and cook for 3–4 minutes. Remove from the heat.
7. To serve, spoon the warm sauce onto four warm serving plates and place two prawns on top of each. Garnish with the lime wedges.

Recipe by Stathis Thermos, executive chef, Santa Marina

SCHLOSS FUSCHL
SALZBURG, AUSTRIA

GLAZED LAKE FUSCHL CHAR WITH BELL PEPPER FOAM, PARSNIP CHERVIL PUREE, AND OSETRA CAVIAR

SERVES 4

For the char:
Olive oil, for coating · 4 ($4^1/_4$-oz) Lake Fuschl char fillets · $1^1/_2$ oz Osetra caviar
Maldon sea salt flakes and freshly ground black pepper, to taste

For the parsnip chervil puree:
10 pieces ($1^4/_5$ lb) parsnip chervil · $2^1/_2$ cups whole milk
7 Tbsp unsalted butter, cubed and very cold
Freshly squeezed lemon juice, to taste
Salt and freshly ground black pepper, to taste

For the bell pepper foam:
$^1/_2$ cup (1 stick) plus $^3/_4$ Tbsp unsalted butter · $1^1/_8$ lb red bell pepper, diced
$3^1/_2$ oz shallots, peeled and diced · 1 Tbsp smoked Spanish paprika
$^1/_3$ cup white wine · $^1/_3$ cup Noilly Prat vermouth · $1^1/_2$ cups fish stock
$^2/_3$ cup heavy cream · $^1/_2$ cup whole milk · $^1/_2$ cup coconut milk · 1 pinch salt
1 pinch freshly ground black pepper · 3 Tbsp cornstarch · Microgreens, for garnish

1. Prepare the char: Preheat the oven to 250°F. Lightly coat a baking sheet with the oil.
2. Glaze the fillets with the oil and place them on the baking sheet. Bake for 8–12 minutes. Remove from the oven. Season with salt and pepper, top each fillet with a quenelle (a small ball) of the caviar, and set aside.
3. Make the puree: Rinse the parsnip chervil in cool water to remove any dirt. Cut off the bottoms and tops, peel, and dice into $^3/_8$-inch pieces.
4. In a saucepan over low heat, warm the milk just until it simmers. Add the chervil, season with salt and pepper, and cook, stirring frequently, for 15–20 minutes, just until softened; drain.
5. Transfer the chervil to a blender and puree for 2–3 minutes, or until smooth, adding milk if needed to reach the proper texture. Add the cold butter and continue to puree for 1 minute. Season with salt and pepper, then add lemon juice to taste.
6. Make the foam: Place a saucepan over medium heat. Using a candy thermometer, heat the butter to 280°F. Add the bell pepper and shallots and braise for 15 minutes. Add the paprika and cook for 15 minutes. Deglaze with the wine and vermouth.
7. Add the fish stock and cook until the volume is reduced by half.

8 Add the cream, milk, coconut milk, salt, and pepper. Simmer for 15–20 minutes, then transfer to a blender.

9 Puree for 8 minutes, then strain through a sieve. Add the cornstarch and stir until the foam reaches the desired consistency.

10 To serve, spoon the puree onto the plate and top with the fish. Top with the caviar and garnish with the microgreens. Spoon the foam around the puree and fish and serve.

Recipe by Johannes Fuchs, executive chef & Julian Schwamberger, chef, Schloss Fuschl

SOFIA HOTEL BALKAN

SOFIA, BULGARIA

SHOPSKA

SERVES 5

3 1/2 medium cucumbers, peeled and diced · 5 1/2 medium tomatoes, diced
2 1/2 large bell peppers, seeded and diced · 2 1/2 oz onion, diced · 3 Tbsp plus 1 tsp vegetable oil
3 Tbsp plus 1 tsp finely chopped fresh parsley, plus more for garnish
8 3/4 oz sheep's milk cheese, freshly grated
3 1/2 oz Dzhulyunska shipka (Bulgarian carrot) chili peppers, baked, for garnish
5 Kalamata olives, for garnish · Finely ground sea salt, to taste

1 In a serving bowl, combine the cucumbers, tomatoes, bell peppers, and onion and toss well. Add the oil and the 3 Tbsp plus 1 tsp parsley, season with salt, and toss again until well combined.

2 Sprinkle with the cheese. Garnish with the chili peppers, olives, and parsley and serve.

Recipe by Desislava Stoyanova, executive chef, Sofia Hotel Balkan

TRUMP TURNBERRY

AYRSHIRE, SCOTLAND

PERTHSHIRE RED DEER CUTLETS, TARRAGON MASHED POTATOES, AND CREAMED CHANTERELLE MUSHROOMS

SERVES 4

For the red deer cutlets:
8 (3½ oz) venison cutlets, trimmed · 1 dash olive oil · 2 cloves garlic, crushed
1 sprig rosemary, coarsely chopped · Sea salt and freshly ground black pepper, to taste

For the tarragon mashed potatoes:
3½ oz double cream or heavy cream · 3 Tbsp unsalted butter
1 lb red rooster potatoes, boiled, peeled, and mashed · 1 Tbsp fresh tarragon, chopped
Sea salt and freshly ground black pepper, to taste

For the creamed chanterelle mushrooms:
¼ cup (½ stick) unsalted butter · 2 shallots, peeled and finely diced · 1 clove garlic, crushed
11 oz chanterelle mushrooms, washed, cleaned with a brush, and trimmed
⅜ cup dry white wine · ⅞ cup heavy cream
Sea salt and freshly ground black pepper, to taste

For serving:
Extra-virgin olive oil, for drizzling

1 Prepare the deer cutlets: Marinate the venison cutlets overnight in the oil, garlic, and rosemary.

2 Heat a grill to 350°F. Season the cutlets with salt and pepper, then grill them for 2 minutes on each side, or until rare. Remove from the grill and cover with foil to keep warm.

3 Make the mashed potatoes: In a saucepan over medium heat, combine the cream and butter and bring to a boil. Remove from the heat.

4 Add the potatoes to the saucepan and stir until well combined. Stir in the tarragon and season with salt and pepper. Set aside.

5 Make the mushrooms: In a saucepan over medium heat, warm the butter. Add the shallots and garlic and cook for 2 minutes. Add the mushrooms and cook gently for 6–7 minutes. Add the wine and cook for 2 minutes, or until the wine evaporates. Add the cream and season with salt and pepper. Remove from the heat.

6 To serve, place the warm mashed potatoes at the top of the plate. Spoon the creamed mushrooms into the center of the plate and lay the deer cutlets on top. Drizzle with the oil and serve.

Recipe by Alan Matthew, executive chef, Trump Turnberry

VEDEMA
SANTORINI, GREECE

SALMON FILLET WITH KATIKI DOMOKOU, SAUTÉED CHERRY TOMATOES, AND MINT OIL

SERVES 4

$1^{3}/_{4}$ lb fresh salmon fillet, cut into 4 portions
$7^{1}/_{4}$ oz Katiki Domokou cheese (a creamy goat cheese produced in northern Greece)
2 Tbsp plus 2 tsp extra-virgin olive oil, divided · $3^{3}/_{4}$ oz cherry tomatoes
2 tsp chopped fresh mint, divided
Sea salt and freshly ground black pepper, to taste

1. Preheat the oven to 350°F.
2. Season the salmon fillets with salt and pepper. In an oven-safe skillet over medium heat, sear the fillets for 2 minutes on each side; place in the oven to keep warm.
3. In a small saucepan over low heat, warm the cheese. Beat for 2 minutes with an electric hand mixer to create foam, doubling the volume of the cheese. Remove from the heat.
4. In the same skillet used for the salmon, over medium heat, warm the 2 tsp of oil. Add the tomatoes and lightly sauté for 30 seconds. Season with salt and pepper and remove from the heat.
5. In a blender, process half of the mint and the remaining 2 Tbsp of oil until creamy.
6. To serve, place the salmon fillets on individual serving plates and drizzle the cheese sauce around them. Distribute the tomatoes among the plates and sprinkle them with the mint oil. Garnish with the remaining mint and additional pepper and serve.

Recipe by Melina Chomata, executive chef, Vedema

THE WELLESLEY KNIGHTSBRIDGE
LONDON, GREAT BRITAIN

LONDON-POLITAN

SERVES 1

$1\frac{1}{3}$ oz vodka · $\frac{1}{2}$ oz Cointreau · 1 Tbsp freshly squeezed lemon juice
$\frac{1}{2}$ tsp blueberry jam · 1 oz cranberry juice · Lime wheel, for garnish

1 In a cocktail shaker filled with ice, combine the vodka, Cointreau, and lemon juice. Using a spoon, dissolve the jam in the cranberry juice and add the mixture to the shaker. Shake until the ingredients are well blended.

2 Double-strain into a large cocktail glass. Garnish with the lime wheel and serve.

"The London-Politan is our interpretation of the traditional Cosmopolitan. We enjoy fusing traditional methods of cocktail making with contemporary hints."

PASQUALE BARTIROMO
bar manager, The Wellesley Knightsbridge

THE WESTBURY
LONDON, GREAT BRITAIN

LOBSTER TOM YUM

SERVES 4

For the tom yum broth:
$1^3/_4$ Tbsp unsalted butter · 1 Tbsp vegetable oil · 1 stalk celery, chopped
1 shallot, peeled and chopped · 1 clove garlic, peeled and chopped
$^1/_4$ medium red chili pepper, chopped · $1^1/_4$ cups vegetable stock, divided
1 stalk lemongrass, chopped · 1 kaffir lime leaf
1 cup freshly grated galangal root or ginger · $1^1/_4$ cups fish stock
$^3/_4$ cup plus 1 Tbsp double cream (or heavy cream) · Maldon sea salt flakes, to taste

For the eggplant and cucumber:
$^1/_2$ eggplant, peeled and cut into $^3/_8$-inch dice
1 cucumber, peeled and cut into $^3/_8$-inch dice
1 Tbsp olive oil · Maldon sea salt flakes, to taste

For the lobster:
Water, to cover · 1 dash vinegar · 6 ($14^1/_2$-oz) live lobsters
1 Tbsp light olive oil · Maldon sea salt flakes, to taste

For serving:
6 button mushrooms, sliced · 2 pieces heart of palm, chopped
Chopped fresh cilantro, to taste · Maldon sea salt flakes, to taste

1 Make the tom yum broth: In a large sauté pan over medium heat, warm the butter and oil. Add the celery, shallot, garlic, and chili pepper and sauté for 6 minutes, or until softened. Add one-third of the vegetable stock, then the lemongrass, lime leaf, and galangal or ginger. Reduce the heat to low and cook for 10 minutes. Add the remaining vegetable stock and the fish stock and cook for 2 minutes, or until the volume is reduced by half. Strain the broth through a fine-mesh sieve and discard the solids.

2 Return the broth to the sauté pan. Add the cream and bring to a boil. Immediately remove from the heat. Season with sea salt and set aside.

3 Make the eggplant and cucumber: In separate bowls, lightly season the eggplant and cucumber with the salt and set aside for 10 minutes. Rinse off the salt and pat the vegetables dry with a cloth.

4 In a sauté pan over medium-high heat, warm the oil. Add the eggplant and lightly sauté for 5–6 minutes, or until it takes on just a little bit of color. Transfer the eggplant to a mixing bowl. Add the cucumber and mix well.

5 Prepare the lobster: In a large pot over high heat, bring the vinegar and enough water to cover the lobsters to a boil. With a sharp knife, pierce the middle of each lobster's head. Add the lobsters to the boiling water and cook for 3 minutes. Remove from the heat. Remove the lobsters from the water and set aside to cool to room temperature.

6 Once the lobsters have cooled, remove the meat and discard the shells. In a sauté pan over medium-high heat, warm the oil. Add the lobster meat and season with sea salt. Cook for about 5 minutes, or until golden on all sides. Remove the meat from the pan and cut it into small dice.

7 Set the tom yum broth over low heat and warm it through.

8 To serve, spoon a little of the eggplant-cucumber mixture onto four serving plates and place a little of the lobster meat on top of it. In four serving bowls, layer equal portions of the remaining lobster meat, eggplant-cucumber mixture, button mushrooms, hearts of palm, and cilantro. Pour the warm broth into the bowls and serve.

LATIN AMERICA

Outdoor dining at Hotel Paracas, Paracas, Peru

HACIENDA PUERTA CAMPECHE
CAMPECHE, MEXICO

PULLED PORK SALBUTE

SERVES 8

1½ cups cooking oil · ½ lb masa
1 tsp salt, plus more to taste · 1 red onion, finely diced
¼ cup freshly squeezed sour orange juice (or ¼ cup combined orange and lime juices)
½ cup cane vinegar · 2 bay leaves · 1 pinch oregano · 8 leaves romaine lettuce
½ lb cochinita pibil (cooked pulled pork) · 1 tomato, sliced
1 avocado, pitted and sliced · Freshly ground black pepper, to taste

1. In a large, heavy pot with high sides over high heat, warm the oil.
2. In a mixing bowl, combine the masa and the 1 tsp of salt with ¼ cup of water. Mix with a spoon until it forms a dough. Using a tortilla press, press the dough into eight tortillas, each slightly smaller than the size of a regular taco.
3. Drop each of the tortillas into the hot oil and fry for 4 minutes, or until thoroughly cooked and inflated. Transfer the tortillas to a paper towel–lined plate to drain.
4. Add the onion to the orange juice and set aside to marinate.
5. In a small saucepan over medium-high heat, combine the vinegar, bay leaves, and oregano. Season with salt and pepper and bring to a boil. Discard the bay leaves. Pour over the marinating onions and set aside to cool completely.
6. To serve, place a piece of the romaine lettuce on top of each fried tortilla. Add an equal amount of the cochinita pibil to each serving. Top with 1 slice of the tomato, 1 slice of the avocado, and an equal portion of the marinated onions and serve.

“In Campeche, amazing culinary secrets are kept–one of them is the famous *salbutes* that explode on a guest's palate. *Salbutes* can also be served with turkey or roasted chicken.”

IGNACIO BAÑUELOS
executive chef, Hacienda Puerta Campeche

COCHINITA PIBIL SHOW

All visitors to the Yucatán should taste the culinary delights of a typical Yucatecan kitchen. One dish especially representative of this region's culture is the *cochinita pibil*: pork flavored in achiote and sour orange. The meat is covered in banana leaves and cooked in an oven built into the ground, giving it a special flavor. Guests at the Haciendas can partake in the *cochinita pibil* cooking show, preparing the dish directly with the chef and enjoying it afterward, served with marinated onion in handmade tortillas.

The experience is a symbol of the region's rich culture and heritage.

HACIENDA SAN JOSE
TIXKOKOB, MEXICO

PAPADZULES

SERVES 4

10 large hard-boiled eggs · 5 fresh tomatoes · 1 white onion, sliced, divided
3 cloves garlic, divided · 2 pieces ($3\frac{1}{4}$ oz) raw habanero pepper
3 Tbsp epazote (a fine Mexican herb) · $\frac{1}{2}$ lb pumpkin seeds, ground
2 Tbsp olive oil · 16 handmade corn tortillas · 1 avocado, sliced, for topping
4 roasted habanero peppers, sliced, for topping · Epazote leaves, for topping
Salt and freshly ground black pepper, to taste

1. Preheat the oven to 350°F. Line a baking sheet with parchment paper.
2. Separate the yolks from the whites of the hard-boiled eggs and crumble them both. Set aside.
3. On the baking sheet, place the tomatoes, 1 slice of the onion, and ½ a clove of the garlic. Season with salt and pepper and roast for 20 minutes. Remove from the oven.
4. Transfer the roasted tomatoes, onion, and garlic to a blender and puree until smooth. Transfer the mixture to a large skillet over medium heat and add the habanero. Bring to a boil. Cook for 4 minutes, or until the sauce thickens. Remove from the heat.
5. In a separate saucepan, bring 4⅛ cups of water to a boil. Add the epazote and boil for 10 minutes, or until the water turns green; transfer to a blender.
6. Add the pumpkin seeds, the remaining onions and garlic, and the oil to the blender and puree for 8 minutes.
7. To serve, fill each of the handmade tortillas with equal amounts of the crumbled egg whites and roll them up. Pour the epazote sauce, over them, then the tomato sauce. Top with the crumbled yolks, avocado, roasted habaneros, and epazote leaves and serve.

HACIENDA SANTA ROSA
SANTA ROSA, MEXICO

SOPA DE LIMA

SERVES 4

1 Tbsp olive oil · 1/2 lb red bell pepper, julienned
1/2 lb green bell pepper, julienned · 1/2 lb yellow bell pepper, julienned
1 white onion, julienned · 2 cups chicken broth · 2 fresh tomatoes, diced
2 Tbsp freshly squeezed lime juice · 1/3 lb cooked chicken breast, shredded or chopped
6 fried tortillas, julienned · Lime slices, for garnish

1 In a frying pan over medium heat, warm the oil. Add the bell peppers and onion and cook for 5 minutes, or until softened. Add the broth and tomatoes and bring to a boil. Add the lime juice and immediately remove from the heat.

2 In a serving bowl, combine the chicken breast and fried tortillas. Pour the soup over the top, garnish with a slice of lime, and serve.

“Considered a flagship dish of the Yucatán Peninsula, lime soup is simple and comforting. Soft but with a rich taste, it is ideal to begin a Yucatecan feast. We suggest enjoying it with homemade tortillas and traditional habanero sauce.”

IGNACIO BAÑUELOS
executive chef, Hacienda Santa Rosa

HACIENDA TEMOZON
TEMOZON SUR, MEXICO

MAYAN FIREFLY

SERVES 1

For the cinnamon and agave infusion:
3 cups agave syrup · 5 cinnamon sticks, broken into pieces

For the Mayan Firefly:
2 oz tequila blanco · $1^1/_2$ oz fresh pineapple juice
$^3/_4$ oz freshly squeezed lemon juice · $^3/_4$ oz Cinnamon and Agave Infusion (above)
1 slice jalapeño pepper, for garnish · Pineapple leaves, for garnish

1 Make the infusion: In a saucepan over low heat, combine the agave syrup, cinnamon sticks, and 1½ cups of water. Bring to a boil, then set aside to cool to room temperature.

2 Make the cocktail: In a cocktail shaker filled with ice, combine the tequila, pineapple and lemon juices, and agave syrup infusion and shake well. Pour into an Old Fashioned glass, garnish with the slice of jalapeño and the pineapple leaves, and serve.

HACIENDA UAYAMON
UAYAMON, MEXICO

HA'ZIKIL P'AK

SERVES 4

2 Tbsp lard · 2 tomatoes, diced · 1 cup pumpkin seeds
1/2 cup chopped white onion · 1 clove garlic, crushed · 1/2 cup chicken broth
1/4 cup sour orange juice · 1 bunch fresh cilantro, chopped, divided
Edam cheese, sliced into shavings, for serving · Corn tortilla chips, for serving
Salt and freshly ground black pepper, to taste

1. In a frying pan over low heat, warm the lard. Add the tomatoes, pumpkin seeds, onion, and garlic and season with salt and pepper. Cook for 10 minutes.
2. Add the broth, orange juice, and all but 2 Tbsp of the cilantro and combine. Remove from the heat.
3. Shape the mixture into 4 quenelles (elegant oval scoops) and place on serving plates. Garnish with the remaining cilantro leaves and serve with the cheese shavings and tortilla chips.

HOTEL PARACAS
PARACAS, PERU

PISCO AND OCTOPUS

SERVES 4

For the quebranta vinaigrette (makes $\frac{1}{2}$ cup):
2 Tbsp plus 2 tsp quebranta pisco (a Peruvian brandy) · 2 Tbsp plus 2 tsp olive oil
3 tsp freshly squeezed lemon juice · 3 tsp vinegar

For the octopus:
1 ($2\frac{1}{4}$-lb) octopus, cleaned · 3 Tbsp quebranta pisco
3 Tbsp paprika · 1 Tbsp olive oil · $\frac{1}{2}$ tsp salt

For the sweet potatoes:
$1\frac{1}{3}$ cups chopped sweet potato · 3 Tbsp olive oil · Salt, to taste

For the salad:
$\frac{3}{4}$ cup chopped red cabbage · $\frac{2}{3}$ cup peeled and chopped green apple
$\frac{3}{8}$ cup chopped radish · $\frac{1}{4}$ cup peeled and chopped cucumber
$\frac{1}{2}$ cup Quebranta Vinaigrette (above) · Salt, to taste

1. Make the quebranta vinaigrette: In a small bowl, combine all the ingredients and whisk until well blended. Set aside.
2. Prepare the octopus: In a large pot over medium heat, bring 5 cups of water to a boil. Add the octopus and boil for 35 minutes.
3. Drain the octopus, cut off the tentacles, and coat them with the pisco, paprika, oil, and salt. Transfer the tentacles to a griddle over medium heat or to a hot grill and cook for 15 seconds, or just until heated through. Transfer to a serving platter and cover with foil to keep warm.
4. Make the sweet potatoes: In a large pot over medium heat, bring 5 cups of water to a boil. Add the sweet potatoes and boil for 20 minutes.
5. Drain the sweet potatoes, then transfer them to a blender. Add the oil and season with salt. Blend until smooth. Transfer to a serving dish and cover with foil to keep warm.
6. Make the salad: In a large serving bowl, combine the cabbage, apple, radish, and cucumber. Toss until combined.
7. To serve, pour the vinaigrette over the salad, season with salt, and toss. Serve with the octopus tentacles and sweet potatoes.

Recipe by Miguel Pulache, executive chef, Hotel Paracas

LAS ALCOBAS
MEXICO CITY, MEXICO

BLOODY OAXACAN

SERVES 1

For the ginger simple syrup (makes enough for 24 cocktails):
1 cup granulated sugar · 3/4 cup freshly grated ginger

For the hibiscus concentrate and foam (makes enough for 24 cocktails):
5 1/2 oz hibiscus flowers

For the Bloody Oaxacan:
6 oz Hibiscus Concentrate (above) · 3 oz fresh pineapple juice · 2 oz Mezcal Espadín
1 oz Ginger Simple Syrup (above) · 1 oz freshly squeezed lime juice
1/4 tsp grated jalapeño pepper · 1/4 tsp freshly grated ginger · 1/2 tsp granulated sugar
2 oz Hibiscus Foam (above) · Jalapeño pepper, sliced, for garnish · Pineapple leaf, for garnish

1 Make the ginger simple syrup: In a small saucepan over medium heat, combine the sugar, ginger, and 3¼ cups of water. Cook for 30 minutes, stirring until the sugar has dissolved. Set aside to cool to room temperature.

2 Make the hibiscus concentrate: In a small saucepan over low heat, combine the hibiscus flowers with 2 cups of water. Cook until the volume is reduced by about half. Remove from the heat.

3 Make the hibiscus foam: Place the hibiscus concentrate in a large container and, using an immersion blender, blend until the mixture foams.

4 Make the cocktail: In a cocktail shaker filled with ice, combine all the liquid ingredients and the grated pepper, ginger, and sugar. Shake and strain into an Old Fashioned glass and top with the hibiscus foam. Garnish with the slices of jalapeño and the pineapple leaf.

Recipe by Alejandro Blanco, head barman and sommelier, Las Alcobas

PALACIO DEL INKA
CUSCO, PERU

CHICHERITO

SERVES 1

For the purple corn-, cinnamon stick-, and Andean mint-infused pisco:
2 oz raw purple corn, trimmed from the ear · 1 cinnamon stick
10 sprigs Andean mint · 45 oz pisco (a Peruvian brandy)

For the quinoa syrup (makes 15 oz):
1 1/8 cups cooked quinoa · 1/2 cup granulated sugar
6 mint leaves · 2 cloves · 1 cinnamon stick

For the simple syrup (makes about 2 cups):
2 1/2 cups granulated sugar

For the foam (makes 6 Tbsp):
15 oz Andean Mint-Infused Pisco (above) · 1 oz Quinoa Syrup (above)
1/2 oz Simple Syrup (above) · 1 egg white

For the Chicherito:
2 oz Purple Corn-Infused Pisco (above) · 2 oz Pisco-Infused Cinnamon Stick (above)
3 oz passion fruit juice · 1/2 oz Simple Syrup (above) · 6 ice cubes
6 Tbsp Foam (above) · 2 small cinnamon sticks, for garnish
6 prickly pear seeds, for garnish · 1 mint leaf, for garnish

1 Make the purple corn- and cinnamon stick-infused pisco: In a tightly sealed container, combine the purple corn and 15 oz of pisco. In a separate tightly sealed container, combine the cinnamon stick and 15 oz of pisco. Set both containers aside for 15 days to infuse.

2 Make the Andean mint-infused pisco: In a tightly sealed container, combine the mint and 15 oz of pisco and set aside for 2 days to infuse.

3 Make the quinoa syrup: In a medium pot over medium heat, combine the cooked quinoa, sugar, and ¾ cup plus 1½ Tbsp of water and bring to a boil. Add the mint, cloves, and cinnamon stick and cook for about 15 minutes, then set aside to cool. Discard the mint, cloves, and cinnamon stick. Place the boiled quinoa in a blender and puree for 20 seconds, or until smooth. Drain using a fine-mesh sieve and set aside.

4 Make the simple syrup: In a pot over medium-high heat, combine the sugar and 2 cups plus 1½ Tbsp of water and bring to a boil. Cook, stirring, until the sugar has dissolved. Set aside to cool.

5 Make the foam: In a blender, combine all the ingredients and blend for 10 seconds.

6 Make the cocktail: In a cocktail shaker, combine the purple corn-infused pisco, cinnamon stick-infused pisco, passion fruit juice, simple syrup, and ice cubes and shake for 15 seconds. Pour into an Old Fashioned glass. Garnish with the foam, cinnamon sticks, prickly pear seeds, and mint leaf and serve.

PALACIO DEL INKA
CUSCO, PERU

PISCO SOUR CLASS

Palacio del Inka's bartenders teach guests all the steps to making an authentic Pisco Sour. This national drink is an essential part of the Peruvian identity, and guests will explore its history in front of Cusco's majestic, original Incan wall—the perfect setting to indulge the senses with the city's best pisco.

From left: Chicherito; Cuatros Bustos courtyard at Palacio del Inka.

PARK TOWER
BUENOS AIRES, ARGENTINA

GREENS, VEGETABLE TEXTURES, AND RASPBERRY SALAD

SERVES 10

For the vinaigrette:
7¼ oz fresh raspberries · ⅓ cup red wine vinegar · 1 cup extra-virgin olive oil

For the beets:
1⅛ lb beets, peeled · 1½ cups plus 3 Tbsp all-purpose flour · 3 large egg whites

For the eggplants:
2 baby eggplants · Olive oil, as needed · ¼ cup chopped fresh rosemary

For the salad:
1 Tbsp olive oil · 5 cups (1 lb) sliced fennel bulb, cut into segments
¼ cup chopped fresh thyme · 5–7 cloves garlic, minced
6⅓ cups (1⅛ lb) mixed greens · 10 cherry tomatoes · ¾ cup sunflower seeds

1 Make the vinaigrette: In a large bowl, muddle the raspberries. Add the vinegar and stir. While whisking constantly, gradually drizzle in the oil. Set aside.

2 Prepare the beets: In a large pot, add the beets and enough water to cover them by 1½–2 inches. Remove the beets, place the pot over high heat, and bring the water to a boil. Reduce the heat to medium-low, add the beets back to the pot, and cook for 20 minutes, or until tender. If the beets are not yet tender, add more water to cover and continue to cook until tender. Remove the beets from the pot (reserve the cooking liquid); transfer them to a blender and process until smooth.

3 Using a fine-mesh sieve, strain the contents of the blender into a microwavable bowl. Stir the flour and egg whites into the processed beets and microwave on high for 1 minute. The mixture will resemble a sponge cake; remove it from the bowl and set aside to cool completely. Once cool, cut the cake-like beets into chunks.

4 Prepare the eggplants: Preheat the oven to 350°F. Line a baking sheet with parchment paper.

5 Place the eggplants on the baking sheet, drizzle them with the oil, and scatter the rosemary over them. Roast for 30 minutes, or until browned. Remove from the oven.

6 Make the salad: In a frying pan over medium-high heat, warm the oil. Add the fennel, thyme, and garlic and sauté for 2 minutes. Remove from the heat.

7 To serve, arrange the greens in a large bowl. Place the cake-like beet chunks, roasted eggplants, sautéed fennel, tomatoes, and sunflower seeds on top of the greens. Drizzle the vinaigrette over the salad and serve.

JAVIER GONZALES ALEMAN

executive chef, Park Tower, Buenos Aires, Argentina

YOUR FAVORITE LOCAL PLACE TO EAT?

My mother's house.

WHAT DO YOU REQUEST THERE?

I make no requests; I just enjoy whatever she has prepared for me.

THE BEST SPOT FOR A COCKTAIL?

My backyard.

WHAT MAKES THIS LOCATION MEMORABLE?

The atmosphere, fresh air, and loved ones around.

YOUR FAVORITE INGREDIENT TO USE IN COOKING?

Seafood and fish.

IN WHICH RECIPES DO THESE INGREDIENTS WORK BEST?

In any recipe that respects the product, avoiding excessive manipulation!

YOUR FAVORITE DISH TO PREPARE?

Spanish paella!

WHAT IS A DISH NO ONE SHOULD VISIT BUENOS AIRES WITHOUT EATING?

Grilled beef.

YOUR PREFERRED COMFORT FOOD?

Homemade pasta, grandma's style!

SAN CRISTOBAL TOWER
SANTIAGO, CHILE

VALVERT GUMER COCTEL

SERVES 1

2 oz 40% double-distilled pisco (a Peruvian brandy) · 1½ oz passion fruit juice
1½ oz pineapple juice · 1 dash Jägermeister (a German digestif)
1 pineapple wedge, for garnish · 1 pineapple leaf, for garnish
1 maraschino cherry, for garnish

1 In a cocktail shaker filled with plenty of ice, combine all the liquid ingredients and shake vigorously for 5–7 seconds.

2 Strain into a short glass with ice, garnish with the pineapple wedge, pineapple leaf, and cherry, and serve.

TAMBO DEL INKA

URUBAMBA, PERU

QUINOA SALAD

SERVES 4

For the quinoa salad:

2 cups quinoa · 3 broccoli florets · 3 cauliflower florets · ¼ cup green beans
8 cherry tomatoes · 4 ears baby corn · 4 baby carrots · ¼ cup sliced radish
16 muña (an herb indigenous to the Andes, similar to mint) leaves, or to taste
3 tsp freshly squeezed lemon juice, or to taste
16 edible flowers, for garnish · Freshly ground black pepper, to taste

For the dressing:

15 muña leaves · 2 tsp freshly squeezed lemon juice
Salt and freshly ground black pepper, to taste · 2 Tbsp olive oil

1 Prepare the quinoa: In a large saucepan over medium-high heat, bring 1 quart of water to a boil and add the quinoa. Cook at a constant boil for 15 minutes, or until softened. Drain, then transfer to a serving bowl. Set aside to cool to room temperature.

2 Prepare the vegetables: In a large lidded pot fitted with a steamer insert, bring 1 inch of water to a boil. Place the broccoli and cauliflower florets, green beans, tomatoes, corn, carrots, and radish in the steamer insert, cover, and steam for 4 minutes. Remove from the heat.

3 Add the muña leaves and lemon juice to the quinoa, then season with salt and pepper. Add the steamed vegetables and stir to combine.

4 Make the dressing: In a measuring cup, combine the muña leaves and lemon juice, then season with salt and pepper. While whisking constantly, gradually drizzle in the oil.

5 To serve, garnish the quinoa with the edible flowers and serve with the dressing.

Milk Chocolate and Strawberries
The Ballantyne, Charlotte, North Carolina
Recipe on pages 166–67

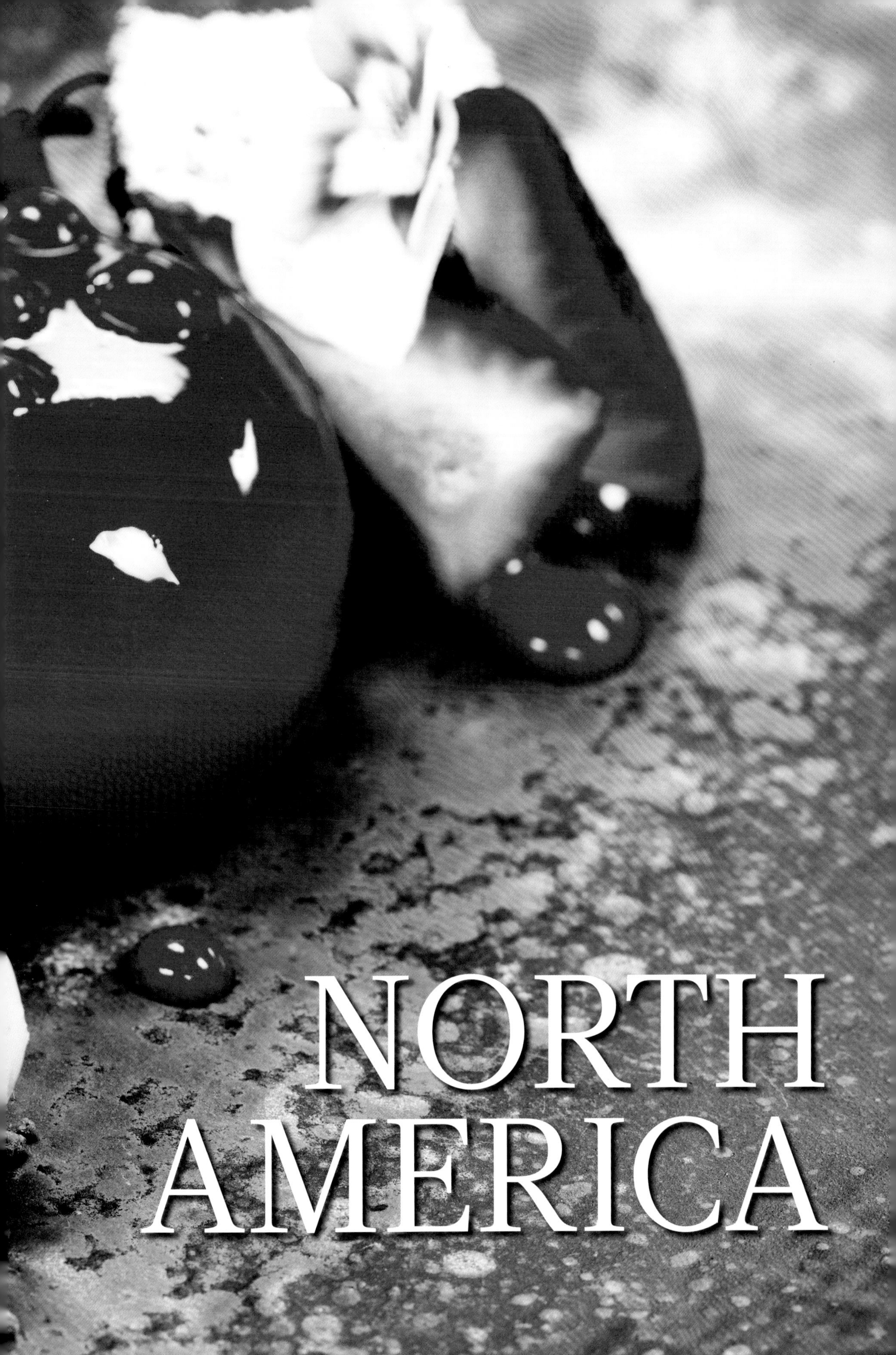
NORTH
AMERICA

THE BALLANTYNE
CHARLOTTE, NORTH CAROLINA, USA

MILK CHOCOLATE AND STRAWBERRIES

SERVES 10

For the pickled strawberries:
1½ lb fresh strawberries, washed, hulled, and sliced in half · 2 sprigs thyme
½ cup apple cider vinegar · 1¼ Tbsp granulated sugar · 1 tsp salt · ¼ cup hot water

For the vanilla sauce (makes 12 oz):
½ cup whole milk · ½ cup heavy cream · ½ vanilla bean, split and seeded
3 large egg yolks · ¼ cup granulated sugar

For the Bavarian cream:
6 sheets gelatin · 12 oz Vanilla Sauce (above) · 7 oz Valrhona Bahibe milk chocolate, melted
1¾ cups heavy cream, whipped into soft peaks

For the neutral glaze (makes 3½ oz):
½ sheet gelatin · ¼ cup granulated sugar · 1 Tbsp cornstarch · 1 Tbsp corn syrup

For the shiny red glaze:
7 sheets gelatin · 2 cups granulated sugar · ½ cup liquid glucose
¾ cup whole milk · ½ cup nonfat dry milk powder
3½ oz Neutral Glaze (above) · ¼ cup olive oil · Red food coloring, as needed

For the chocolate pound cake:
1 cup (2 sticks) unsalted butter · 3 cups confectioners' sugar
1½ cups almond flour · 1 cup all-purpose flour
¼ cup unsweetened Dutch-process cocoa powder · 1 Tbsp baking powder
14 large egg whites · 2 Tbsp Trimoline (invert sugar) or corn syrup · 1 tsp vanilla paste

For serving:
Chocolate ice cream

1 Make the pickled strawberries: In a large bowl, combine the strawberries and thyme. In a small saucepan over medium-high heat, combine the vinegar, sugar, salt, and hot water. Simmer for 10 minutes, or until the sugar and salt have dissolved. Pour the mixture over the strawberries and thyme. Set aside to cool to room temperature, then refrigerate overnight.

2 Make the vanilla sauce: In a small saucepan over medium-high heat, bring the milk, cream, vanilla pod, and seeds to a boil. In a mixing bowl, whisk together the yolks and sugar until lightened. While whisking constantly, gradually pour the hot cream mixture, little by little, into the yolks. After half of the hot cream mixture has been added, pour the contents of the bowl back into the saucepan. Cook, stirring constantly, over medium heat for 8 minutes, or until the mixture is thickened and coats the back of a spoon. Strain into a clean bowl, then set in an ice bath to cool.

3 Make the Bavarian cream: Soften the gelatin sheets by placing them in a bowl of cold water. When softened, remove the gelatin, squeeze out the excess water, and set aside.

4 In a medium saucepan over medium-low heat, warm the vanilla sauce and softened gelatin until the gelatin has melted, about 5 minutes. Pour the contents of the saucepan over the melted chocolate and stir until thoroughly combined. Set aside to cool to room temperature.

5 Once the chocolate mixture has cooled, fold in the whipped cream. Pour into a silicone mold and freeze overnight.

6 Make the neutral glaze: Soften the gelatin sheet by placing it in a bowl of cold water. When softened, remove the gelatin, squeeze out the excess water, and set aside.

7 In a small saucepan over high heat, combine the sugar and ¼ cup of water and bring to a boil.

8 In a small bowl, stir together the cornstarch and ¼ cup of water.

9 Add the cornstarch mixture to the boiling water. Reduce the heat to medium and cook, stirring often, for about 5 minutes, or until thickened. Remove from the heat and stir in the corn syrup. Return to medium-high heat and bring to a boil. Remove from the heat, add the softened gelatin, stir well to combine, and set aside to cool.

10 Make the shiny red glaze: Soften the gelatin sheets by placing them in a bowl of cold water. When softened, remove the gelatin, squeeze out the excess water, and set aside.

11 In a medium saucepan over high heat, combine the sugar, glucose, and ⅓ cup of water and bring to a boil.

12 In a mixing bowl, combine the milk and milk powder. Slowly add the milk mixture to the saucepan containing the sugar mixture, bring back to a boil, and cook for 2 minutes. Remove from the heat.

13 Add the softened gelatin, neutral glaze, oil, and food coloring, as desired, to the saucepan and blend using an immersion blender until thoroughly combined. Set the glaze aside to cool to 95°F. Meanwhile, carefully unmold the frozen Bavarian cream, then pour the cooled glaze over it to coat it completely.

14 Make the chocolate pound cake: Preheat the oven to 350°F. In a medium saucepan over medium-high heat, melt the butter until it foams and begins to boil. Reduce the heat to medium and swirl the butter occasionally, but do not stir. When the butter takes on a toasty brown color and has a nutty aroma, immediately pour it into a heatproof bowl and set aside to cool to room temperature.

15 In the bowl of a stand mixer fitted with the paddle attachment, combine the sugar, flours, cocoa, and baking powder. Add the egg whites, Trimoline, and vanilla paste and mix on low speed until combined. Add the melted butter and mix again on low speed until combined.

16 Pour the batter into a 9-by-13-inch cake pan and bake for 20 minutes. Transfer to a rack to cool to room temperature. Once cooled, slice the cake into 1-inch cubes.

17 To serve, place the glazed Bavarian cream at the center left of a serving platter. Add the cubes of chocolate pound cake in the center in a line with the Bavarian cream in the middle. Place the pickled strawberries on and around the cakes, as desired. Serve with the ice cream.

Recipe by Benjamin Kallenbach, executive pastry chef, The Ballantyne

THE CANYON SUITES AT THE PHOENICIAN
SCOTTSDALE, ARIZONA, USA

2704'

SERVES 1

For the rosemary-infused mesquite honey (makes 4½ cups):
3 cups Arizona mesquite desert honey · ½ cups purified water · 4 sprigs rosemary

For the 2704':
1½ oz Phoenician Woodford Reserve bourbon · 1 oz Domaine de Canton ginger liqueur
¾ oz Rosemary-Infused Mesquite Honey (above)
½ oz freshly squeezed lemon juice · 2 dashes Fee Brothers lemon bitters
3 large sprigs rosemary · Candied lemon wheel, for garnish

1 Make the rosemary-infused mesquite honey: In a pan over low heat, combine the honey and purified water. While the mixture is heating, whisk until fully blended.

2 When the liquid is warm, add the rosemary and let steep for 10 minutes. Strain to remove any rosemary particles and place in a container until completely cooled.

3 Make the cocktail: In a cocktail shaker filled with ice, combine all the liquid ingredients and 2 rosemary sprigs. Shake vigorously until chilled, then double-strain over a large ice cube in a rocks glass. Garnish with the third rosemary sprig pierced through a candied lemon wheel and serve.

"Named after the peak elevation of Camelback Mountain, the formation The Canyon Suites nestles against, this cocktail is made with The Phoenician's private select Woodford Reserve bourbon and locally sourced mesquite honey, honoring our Sonoran Desert surroundings."

JARED SOWINSKI
beverage director, Canyon Suites at the Phoenician

THE CHATWAL

NEW YORK, NY, USA

ATLANTIC COBIA CRUDO

SERVES 6

$^1/_4$ cup Sicilian pistachios · 1 (10-oz) fillet sushi-grade Atlantic cobia, cleaned, boned, and cut into 30 $^1/_8$-inch-thick slices · 1 Tbsp extra-virgin olive oil
Finely grated zest and freshly squeezed juice of $^1/_2$ a pink grapefruit
$^1/_2$ oz white sturgeon caviar · 1 fresh Fresno chili pepper, thinly sliced into 30 pieces
1 black radish, thinly sliced into 30 pieces · Maldon sea salt flakes, to taste

1. In a medium saucepan, bring the pistachios to a boil in enough water to cover them by at least 1 inch. Cook for about 10 minutes, or until the nuts are tender. Strain the nuts and reserve the liquid.
2. Transfer the nuts to a blender and puree, gradually adding the reserved cooking liquid to create an emulsion. When completely smooth, season with sea salt and transfer to a piping bag.
3. Arrange the cobia slices (5 per serving) on a piece of parchment paper. Lightly brush each slice with the oil and season with sea salt. Scatter a small amount of the zest and then a sprinkle of the juice, to balance the flavors, over all the slices.
4. Curl each cobia slice into a tight roll and top each with a small squeeze of the pistachio puree and a small amount of the sturgeon caviar. Garnish each roll with a slice of chili pepper and a thin disk of the radish and serve.

SOPHIE ELGORT

photographer

YOUR FAVORITE LOCAL PLACE TO EAT?

Indochine on Lafayette Street in NoHo.

YOUR BEST MEAL THERE?

Summer rolls and Chilean sea bass.

WHAT DISH WILL YOU TRAVEL ACROSS THE WORLD TO EAT?

Norwegian rømmegrøt, aka porridge made with sour cream, with cinnamon sugar sprinkled on top.

YOUR FAVORITE FOOD AND DRINK PAIRING?

Cheese and red wine.

THE BEST QUALITY ABOUT THE LOCAL CUISINE?

The diversity of what you can get in a one-block radius all across New York City.

WHAT DISH REMINDS YOU OF HOME?

My family's traditional go-to brunch: bialys, bagels, smoked salmon, sable, cream cheese, and fresh-squeezed orange juice.

YOUR PREFERRED COMFORT FOOD?

Ice cream.

THE EQUINOX
MANCHESTER VILLAGE, VERMONT, USA

BLACK KALE SALAD WITH SMOKED MAPLE VINAIGRETTE

SERVES 4

For the smoked maple vinaigrette:
4 shallots, peeled and roughly chopped · 1/2 cup maple vinegar
1/2 cup smoked maple syrup · 2 Tbsp Dijon mustard · 1 1/2 cups canola oil
Salt and freshly ground black pepper, to taste

For the kale salad:
2 bunches Tuscan kale · 4 oz Cambozola Black Label cheese (a German blue cheese)
2 oz macadamia nuts, toasted · 2 oz butternut squash, diced and roasted
2 oz bacon lardons, oven-baked · Sea salt and freshly ground black pepper, to taste

1 Make the vinaigrette: In a blender, combine the shallots, maple vinegar, maple syrup, and mustard and blend for 1 minute, or until smooth. Slowly add the oil while the blender is running, forming an emulsion. Season with salt and pepper.

2 Make the salad: In a mixing bowl, combine the kale, cheese, nuts, and squash. Add the vinaigrette and mix thoroughly. Set aside for 15–20 minutes to allow the kale to soften. Season with salt and pepper, top with the lardons, and serve.

Recipe by Daniel Black, executive chef, The Equinox

THE GWEN
CHICAGO, ILLINOIS, USA

CREOLE MAPLE OLD FASHIONED

SERVES 1

$1^{1}/_{2}$ oz Koval rye whiskey · $^{1}/_{2}$ oz Clement Créole Shrubb orange liqueur
$^{1}/_{4}$ oz maple syrup · 2 dashes orange bitters · Orange peel, for garnish
Luxardo maraschino cherry, for garnish

1 In a mixing glass, combine all ingredients and stir. Pour into a rocks glass over 1 large ice cube.

2 Garnish with the orange peel and cherry and serve.

“A refined take on the classic Whiskey Old Fashioned and newly popular Rum Old Fashioned. We selected this rye whiskey because it is locally distilled in Chicago. The drink starts with a tart orange bite followed by a smooth and sweet maple finish.”

THE CULINARY TEAM
The Gwen

HOTEL IVY

MINNEAPOLIS, MINNESOTA, USA

CONSTANTINE OLD FASHIONED

SERVES 1

2 oz Constantine Select Knob Creek bourbon · 1/4 oz Earl Giles piloncillo syrup
1 dash Bitter Truth chocolate bitters · 1 dash Earl Giles sarsaparilla bitters
1 dash Regan's orange bitters · Orange peel, for garnish
1 Luxardo maraschino cherry, for garnish

1. In a mixing glass, combine the bourbon; piloncillo syrup; and chocolate, sarsaparilla, and orange bitters. Add crushed ice and stir rapidly for proper dilution.
2. Strain over fresh hand-chipped ice into a lowball or Old Fashioned glass.
3. Garnish with the orange peel and cherry and serve.

"Even though our Old Fashioned recipe never changes, the variance of flavor from year to year in the bourbon barrel does, which means the Old Fashioned is never old."

JESSE HELD
head bartender, Hotel Ivy

HOTEL TALISA
VAIL, COLORADO, USA

PHEASANT SOUP

SERVES 10

1 gallon room-temperature water · 1 Nueske's applewood smoked whole pheasant
1 Spanish onion, halved · 1/2 bunch celery · 1/4 cup chopped fresh thyme
1/2 Tbsp black peppercorns · 2 cups diced Spanish onion · 2 cups diced celery
2 cups corn, roasted · 1 cup (2 sticks) unsalted butter · 3 cups heavy cream
1 cup sherry wine · 1 cup apple juice · 2 Tbsp apple cider vinegar
2 tsp sherry wine vinegar · 1 tsp Worcestershire sauce · Tabasco, to taste
1/4 cup cornstarch · 1/2 cup wild rice, cooked · Kosher salt and white pepper, to taste

1. Make the stock: In a large pot over medium heat, combine the water, pheasant, halved onion, celery, thyme, and peppercorns and simmer for 2 hours. Add more water, if needed, to keep the pheasant submerged.
2. Remove the pheasant from the pot and open it slightly to allow steam to escape. Set it aside for 3–4 minutes.
3. Strain the stock into a large container and discard the solids. Reserve 2–3 quarts of the stock for the soup.
4. Pick the pheasant meat from the bones, being careful that no bones are left in the meat; set aside.
5. In a large, deep sauté pan over medium heat, warm the butter. Add the diced onion, celery, and corn and sauté for 2 minutes. Add 2 quarts of the stock and the cream, sherry, apple juice, apple cider vinegar, sherry vinegar, Worcestershire sauce, and Tabasco. Season with salt and pepper, bring to a simmer, and cook for 2 minutes.
6. In a small bowl, whisk the cornstarch with 1 cup of cold water to make a slurry. Whisk the slurry into the soup. After the soup has thickened, add some or all of the remaining stock to bring it to the desired thickness. If you add more stock, bring the soup back to a simmer for 1 minute. Remove from the heat.
7. To serve, place the cooked rice in a large serving bowl and pour the soup over it.

LAS ALCOBAS

ST. HELENA, CALIFORNIA, USA

HAMACHI CRUDO AND SEBASTOPOL APPLES

SERVES 4

For the apple vinaigrette:
4 Granny Smith apples, washed · 4 jalapeño peppers, washed
1/2 cup Sparrow Lane apple cider vinegar · Sea salt, to taste

For the apple relish:
4 Granny Smith apples, peeled, cored, and finely diced
4 red serrano peppers, seeded and finely diced
4 jalapeño peppers, seeded and finely diced · 1/4 cup extra-virgin olive oil
Freshly squeezed lemon juice, to taste · Kosher salt, to taste

For the crudo:
16–24 oz sashimi-grade hamachi (Pacific yellowtail) · 4 Tbsp extra-virgin olive oil
20 fresh chives, roughly chopped · 20 fresh chive flowers
Extra-virgin olive oil, as needed · Fleur de sel, to taste

1 Make the vinaigrette: Process the apples and jalapeño peppers through a juicer. Capture the juice, whisk in the apple cider vinegar, and season with sea salt. Set aside.

2 Make the relish: In a small mixing bowl, combine the apples, peppers, and oil and mix well Season with the lemon juice and salt. Set aside.

3 Make the crudo: Using a long, sharp chef's knife, cut each hamachi against the grain into 6 ¼-inch-thick slices. Brush well with the oil. Arrange 6 hamachi slices like shingles down the middle of each of the four serving plates and season with the fleur de sel. Spread the apple relish on top of the fish, arrange the chives on the relish, and top with the chive flowers. Pour the apple vinaigrette around the fish and finish with drops of the oil.

Recipe by Thanawat Bates, executive chef, Las Alcobas

CHRIS COSENTINO

executive chef, Las Alcobas, Napa Valley, California, USA

YOUR FAVORITE LOCAL PLACE TO EAT?

I have two favorite spots: Two Birds/One Stone in St. Helena for delicious Japanese-inspired food and unique wines from producers in the area, and Torc in Napa, where the food is always honest and delicious. Chef Sean O'Toole is doing great things there.

WHAT DO YOU ORDER THERE?

At Torc, I let Sean choose for me, since his menu is always changing and he usually has something exciting and new for me to try. At Two Birds, I am a huge fan of their wagyu short rib with Korean BBQ, savory Japanese pancakes, and crispy Sonoma duck leg.

YOUR FAVORITE INGREDIENT TO USE IN COOKING?

I live by using plenty of acid and lots of herbs as bright flavoring agents, before salt.

WHAT IS A DISH NO ONE SHOULD VISIT THIS CITY WITHOUT EATING?

The tripe at Terra is hands down the best. Chef Hiro Stone has that dish perfected. It will convert even the pickiest of diners who thought they didn't like tripe.

YOUR PREFERRED COMFORT FOOD?

I'm a sucker for a perfect plate of pasta, like a simple cacio e pepe or carbonara.

THE LIBERTY
BOSTON, MASSACHUSETTS, USA

PARSNIP FLAN

SERVES 6

For the parsnip puree:
1 parsnip, peeled and cut into small pieces · 5/8 cup whole milk
2 shallots, peeled and minced · 1 clove garlic, peeled and minced
1/2 Tbsp chopped fresh thyme

For the flan:
1 large egg · 2 Tbsp freshly shredded Swiss cheese · 1 recipe Parsnip Puree (above)
Salt and freshly ground black pepper, to taste

1. Make the puree: In a saucepan over medium heat, combine the parsnip, milk, shallots, garlic, and thyme and simmer for 5 minutes, or until the vegetables are tender and translucent. Transfer the mixture to a blender and puree until smooth. Transfer to a bowl and set aside to cool to room temperature.
2. Make the flan: Preheat the oven to 350°F.
3. Whisk the egg and cheese into the parsnip puree and season with salt and pepper.
4. Spray six 4-oz foil cups with nonstick cooking spray and pour the mixture into the cups. Bake in the oven for 30 minutes, or until firm. Transfer to a rack to cool completely before serving.

Recipe by Anthony Dawodu, executive chef, Clink, The Liberty

THE NINES
PORTLAND, OREGON, USA

WILD OREGON MUSHROOMS

SERVES 6–8

For the pickled shallots:
36–48 shallots, peeled and sliced into ¼-inch-thick rings
½ cup red wine vinegar · ½ cup granulated sugar · 1 Tbsp salt

For the mushrooms:
¾ cup grapeseed oil · 48 oz each of chanterelle, hedgehog, and porcini mushrooms, cleaned and cut into even pieces
2 heads garlic, halved horizontally · 10–12 sprigs thyme · 4 Tbsp unsalted butter
Kosher salt and freshly ground black pepper, to taste

For serving:
1 recipe Pickled Shallots (above) · 12 sprigs parsley

1. Make the shallots: In a pot over medium heat, bring the vinegar, sugar, salt, and ½ cup of water to a simmer. Add the shallots to the mixture, remove from the heat, and let stand at room temperature for 10 minutes.
2. Prepare the mushrooms: Coat the bottom of a large sauté pan with the grapeseed oil and place it over high heat until the oil reaches the smoke point. Add a single layer of the mushrooms. Brown the mushrooms on the first side, making sure not to move them too much. When the first side is browned, begin stirring the mushrooms, keeping them spread out evenly. Add the garlic head halves and thyme, allowing them to sizzle in the oil. Add 1 Tbsp of the butter and allow to brown in the pan. Season the mushrooms lightly with salt and pepper (if you season the mushrooms prior to browning, the mushrooms will bleed out their water). Remove from the pan and transfer to a bowl.
3. Repeat the above step with the remaining mushrooms in four batches, until all are cooked and all the butter has been used. Discard the thyme and garlic.
4. Transfer all the cooked mushrooms to a large pan over medium heat. Cook until all the mushrooms are warmed through. Remove from the heat.
5. To serve, transfer the mushrooms to a serving dish. Garnish with the rings of pickled shallot and parsley sprigs and serve.

PALACE HOTEL
SAN FRANCISCO, CALIFORNIA, USA

SPOT PRAWN CEVICHE

SERVES 4–6

For the yucca root chips:
2 quarts canola oil · 6 oz large yucca roots, very thinly sliced

For the spot prawn ceviche:
30 Santa Barbara spot prawns, cooked, shelled, chilled, and cut in half lengthwise (reserve cooked heads of 12–18 of the prawns for serving)
Meat of 1 fresh young coconut, sliced into bite-size pieces
1 manila mango, very finely julienned · 1 ripe avocado, very finely julienned
4–6 kaffir lime leaves, finely cut into slender ribbons
1/4 red onion, very finely julienned · 1/4 cup freshly squeezed lime juice
1 habanero pepper, cut into thin rounds
1/4 Tbsp peeled and finely minced fresh ginger · 1 pinch chopped fresh cilantro
1 pinch chopped fresh mint · Maldon sea salt flakes, to taste

For serving:
1/4 cup bull's blood microgreens · 12–18 cooked spot prawn heads

1. Make the yucca root chips: Place the oil in a deep pot over medium heat. Using a candy thermometer, bring the oil to 270°F. Add the yucca chips and fry for 2–4 minutes, or until crisp. Transfer the chips to paper towel–lined plates to drain.
2. Make the ceviche: In a serving bowl, combine all the ceviche ingredients and lightly toss. Garnish with the microgreens and prawn heads and serve with the yucca root chips.

“Spot prawns are a true California treasure and the key to creating this simple, elegant signature dish befitting of the Palace–it makes a lasting impression.”

JOHN HART
executive chef, Palace Hotel

THE PHOENICIAN
SCOTTSDALE, ARIZONA, USA

SWEET AND SOUR BEET RISOTTO AND MEYER LEMON

SERVES 4

For the herb tea (makes 1 quart):
1 bunch rosemary, broken at the last minute
1 bunch thyme, broken at the last minute · 1 Thai chili pepper, split
1 lemon peel, pith removed · 2 1/2 Tbsp salt

For the risotto:
1 cup extra-virgin olive oil · 1 oz shallot, peeled and minced
4 cups Japanese Nishiki rice · 1 quart Herb Tea (above)

For the baby beets:
Salted water, to cover · 4 baby red beets · 4 baby gold beets
4 baby candy-striped beets · 1 Tbsp olive oil

For the roasted beets:
2 Tbsp olive oil · 1 lb red beets, washed · 2 tsp salt

For the beet marmalade:
1/2 lb Roasted Beets (above), finely diced · 1 cup red wine vinegar
1/2 cup sherry vinegar · 2 1/2 Tbsp granulated sugar
1 oz Bottlegreen Ginger & Lemongrass Cordial · 1 Tbsp salt

For the Meyer lemon foam:
1 cup Meyer lemon juice, strained
7/8 oz Bottlegreen Elderflower Cordial · 1/8 tsp lecithin

For serving:
Chopped fresh chervil, for garnish · Freshly grated Meyer lemon zest, for garnish

1 Make the herb tea: In a large pot over high heat, combine all the ingredients except the salt with 1 quart of water. Using a candy thermometer, bring the mixture to 275°F. Cover and set aside to steep for 30 minutes to steep. Strain through a fine-mesh sieve or chinois and press down on the solids to ensure total extraction of all the liquid. Season with the salt.

2 Make the risotto: In a large sauté pan over high heat, warm the oil. Add the shallot and cook for 5 minutes, or just until tender. Add the rice; cook, stirring constantly with a silicone spatula, for 5 minutes, or until the tips of the rice are translucent. Reduce the heat to medium; add enough of the tea to saturate the rice. Cook, constantly folding the rice over itself, for 10–15 minutes, or until almost dry. Repeat until all the tea has been used. Transfer the risotto to a thin baking sheet, cover with a damp towel, and set aside to cool to room temperature. Keep covered until needed.

3 Prepare the baby beets: In a large pot over medium-high heat, bring the salted water to a boil. Add the baby red beets and cook for 7–10 minutes, or until tender, then set aside to cool. Repeat separately with the baby gold beets and the baby candy-striped beets. When all the baby beets have cooled, peel and discard the skins.

4 In a lidded sauté pan over medium heat, warm the oil. Transfer the peeled beets to the sauté pan and cook for 4 minutes, or until more tender. Remove from the heat and cover to keep warm.

5 Make the roasted beets: Preheat the oven to 275°F. Drizzle the oil over the beets and season with the salt. Wrap the beets in foil, ensuring a tight seal. Place them on a baking sheet and bake for 1 hour and 15 minutes. Remove from the oven. Remove the foil and set the beets aside to cool. Once cool to the touch, peel and discard the skins.

6 Make the beet marmalade: In a large saucepan over medium heat, combine all the ingredients and cook for 15 minutes, or until syrupy. Remove from the heat.

7 Make the lemon foam: In a saucepan over medium heat, warm the lemon juice, elderflower cordial, and ½ cup of water. Add the lecithin and, using an immersion blender, puree well, aerating to attain a dense foam. Set aside to settle for 1 minute. When ready to use, skim the foam from the top.

8 In a large saucepan over high heat, combine the risotto, marmalade, and sautéed baby beets and cook, stirring often, for 3–5 minutes, or until creamy. Remove from the heat.

9 To serve, transfer the contents of the saucepan to a serving dish. Top with the diced roasted beets and sprinkle with the lemon foam. Garnish with the chervil and lemon zest and serve.

THE ROYAL HAWAIIAN
WAIKIKI, HAWAII, USA

MODERN FRUITS DE MER

SERVES 4

For the coconut-yuzu cream:
1 cup Chaokoh coconut milk · 1/4 cup granulated sugar · 1/2 Tbsp kosher salt
1/4 cup peeled and crushed fresh ginger · 1 stalk lemongrass, smashed and bruised
1/2 Tbsp cornstarch · 2 Tbsp yuzu or lime juice

For the coconut-avocado mousse (makes 4 oz):
2 whole avocados, pitted and peeled · 1 cup Coconut-Yuzu Cream (above)
1/2 cup tightly packed fresh spinach · Freshly squeezed juice of 1/2 a lime
1 Tbsp sambal oelek chili paste · 1 tsp kosher salt

For poaching the prawns and lobster:
1 (2-lb) Kona lobster, deveined with shell and head on, cut into 6 pieces
6 colossal (13–15 prawns per pound) Kauai prawns
2 stalks celery, thinly sliced · 1 onion, thinly sliced · 1 carrot, thinly sliced
1 cup white wine · 1/4 cup tarragon vinegar · 1/4 cup kosher salt
Freshly squeezed juice of 1 lemon · 3 sprigs thyme

For marinating the poached prawns and lobster:
Poached Kona Lobster, shell removed (above) · 6 Poached Colossal Kauai Prawns (above)
1/2 cup olive oil · Freshly grated zest of 2 lemons
Salt and freshly ground black pepper, to taste

For the lemon-tarragon soy vinaigrette (makes 2 cups):
3 large egg yolks · 1/4 cup tarragon vinegar · 2 Tbsp Yamasa soy sauce
1 tsp kosher salt · 1 cup grapeseed oil · 1/2 cup olive oil
1/4 cup finely chopped fresh tarragon leaves

For the ginger-soy poke sauce (makes 2 cups):
1 cup soy sauce · 1/4 cup peeled and minced fresh ginger · 2 Tbsp sambal oelek chili paste
1 Tbsp rice vinegar · 2 tsp sesame oil · 1/4 cup granulated sugar

For the spicy ahi tuna:
4 1/2 oz raw ahi (bigeye or yellowfin) tuna, finely diced
4 Tbsp Ginger-Soy Poke Sauce (above)
1 pinch finely chopped fresh chives · Kosher salt, to taste

For the fruits de mer:
4 oz Sumida Farms watercress and frisée salad greens
1/4 cup plus 2 Tbsp Lemon-Tarragon Soy Vinaigrette (above), divided
2 oz Kahuku corn, grilled and cut off the ear · 2 oz hearts of palm, finely diced
2 Tbsp lemon-flavored olive oil · 4 oz Coconut-Avocado Mousse (above)
4 1/2 oz Spicy Ahi Tuna (above) · 3 Tbsp crushed bubu arare or other rice crackers, for garnish
6 Poached and Marinated Kauai Prawns (above)
1 Poached and Marinated Kona lobster (above)
2 Tbsp shiso microgreens, for garnish · Salt, to taste

continued on following page

continued from previous page

1 Make the coconut-yuzu cream: In a saucepan over medium heat, combine all ingredients except the cornstarch and yuzu juice and bring to a boil. Reduce the heat to low and simmer for 10 minutes. In a small bowl, whisk the cornstarch with 1 Tbsp of water to make a slurry. Whisk the slurry into the simmering mixture until it thickens. Fold the yuzu juice into the mixture, then set aside to cool.

2 Make the coconut-avocado mousse: In a powerful blender, combine all the ingredients and puree on medium speed until fully combined, about 3 minutes. Place in a squeeze bottle and refrigerate until needed.

3 Poach the prawns and lobster: In a pot over high heat, combine all the ingredients except the lobster and prawns with ½ gallon of water and bring to a boil. Reduce the heat to low and simmer for 15 minutes. Add the lobster and prawns. Remove from the heat and set aside to allow the lobster and prawns to poach in the liquid for 5–6 minutes. Remove the lobster and prawns from the liquid and set aside to cool.

4 Marinate the poached prawns and lobster: Remove the lobster from its shell. In a mixing bowl, combine the oil and zest and season with salt and pepper. Drizzle this mixture on top of the lobster and prawns to marinate.

5 Make the vinaigrette: In a blender, combine the egg yolks, tarragon vinegar, soy sauce, salt, and ½ cup of water and blend on low speed. While the blender is running, slowly drizzle in the grapeseed and olive oils until the mixture is fully emulsified. As the blender continues to run, slowly add the tarragon leaves. Set aside.

6 Make the ginger-soy poke sauce: In a mixing bowl, combine all the ingredients with ½ cup of water and whisk until fully combined.

7 Make the spicy ahi tuna: In a wide, shallow bowl, season the tuna with the salt to taste. Add the ginger-soy poke sauce and the chives and set aside for 30 minutes to marinate.

8 Make the fruits de mer: In a large serving bowl, toss the watercress and frisée with 2 Tbsp of the vinaigrette.

9 In a small mixing bowl, mix the corn and hearts of palm with the remaining ¼ cup of the vinaigrette.

10 To serve, make a diagonal line of the coconut-avocado mousse on four square serving plates. Place three small dollops of the mousse in a triangle shape around the center of each plate. Place three small piles of the dressed salad greens in between the dollops of mousse. Along the diagonal line of mousse, place three small piles of the dressed corn and hearts of palm. In between these piles, place three piles of the spicy ahi tuna and garnish the ahi with the bubu arare. Place a prawn on top of each pile of salad and place a piece of the lobster on top of each pile of corn and hearts of palm. Garnish the prawns and lobster with the microgreens and serve with the vinaigrette.

Recipe by Colin Hazama, executive chef, The Royal Hawaiian

THE ROYAL HAWAIIAN
WAIKIKI, HAWAII, USA

EPICUREAN JOURNEYS
ROOTS & VINES

The Ocean Lawn at The Royal Hawaiian.

Roots & Vines is inspired by each chef's cultural traditions, passed down through generations, which became the foundation of the multiethnic regional cuisine of Hawaii. The journey begins on Friday with a sunset cocktail reception including wine and amuse-bouches on Azure restaurant's upper deck. Executive chef Colin Hazama and his team present an array of dinner courses showcasing local ingredients such as taro and the *moi* fish, the latter previously only allowed to be enjoyed by *ali'i* (royalty). Certified sommelier Micah Suderman pairs the dishes with complementary New World wines and spirits, and sweet delicacies by executive pastry chef Carolyn Portuondo round out the evening. All dishes are served at a community table, meant to inspire conversation among old friends and new.

On Saturday, continue the experience with an engaging hands-on cooking class and lunch. With guidance from the culinary team, guests will whip up local dishes and learn the secrets of the kitchen to surprise friends and family back home. A grand *hukilau*-style lunch of all the dishes prepared completes the adventure.

SLS HOTEL

BEVERLY HILLS, CALIFORNIA, USA

THE ULTIMATE GIN & TONIC

SERVES 1

1 ice sphere · $2^1/_2$ oz Hendrick's gin · 1 lemon rind · 1 lime wheel
2 juniper berries · 1 sprig lemon verbena
Fever Tree tonic water, to taste, for topping off

1 Place the ice sphere in a glass and pour the gin over it. Place the lemon rind, lime wheel, and juniper berries inside the glass.

2 Add the lemon verbena, top off with the tonic water, and serve.

Recipe by José Andrés, executive chef, SLS Hotel

THE ST. ANTHONY
SAN ANTONIO, TEXAS, USA

TEXAS COWBOY TOMAHAWK STEAK AND GULF SHRIMP

SERVES 8

For the cilantro vinegar:
2 cups chopped fresh cilantro · 1/4 cup white balsamic vinegar
Freshly squeezed juice of 2 limes

For the steaks:
8 (5 1/4 lb) tomahawk (long-bone rib) steaks

For the marinade:
1 cup olive oil · 3/4 cup Cilantro Vinegar (above) · 1/2 cup chopped Mexican oregano
1/4 cup sal con flor de Jamaica (hibiscus flower sea salt) · 2 Tbsp chopped onion
2 Tbsp cracked black peppercorns · 2 tsp cloves · 2 tsp crushed garlic

For the prawns:
4 Gulf prawns, shells on · 1/2 cup (1 stick) salted butter, melted
1/4 cup achiote (annatto) paste
Freshly squeezed juice and finely grated zest of 4 Texas Valley oranges

For the Yukon gold dauphinoise potatoes:
1 cup heavy cream · 2 egg yolks · 2 Tbsp Parmesan cheese
1 tsp white pepper · 2 Yukon gold potatoes, very thinly sliced

For the huitlacoche demi-glace:
3 cups beef demi-glace · 8 oz huitlacoche mushrooms

For serving:
Locally sourced serrano peppers, heirloom baby tomatoes, and sage, for garnish

1. Make the cilantro vinegar: Combine all the ingredients in a small bowl. Set aside.
2. Prepare the steaks: In a smoker, warm 1 cup of mesquite wood chips. Place the steaks in the smoker and leave them in until the chips are no longer smoking. Remove from the smoker.
3. Make the marinade: Combine all the ingredients in a container large enough to hold all the steaks. Stir until well combined. Transfer the steaks to the marinade and refrigerate overnight.
4. Prepare the prawns: Butterfly-cut the prawns and skewer them to prevent the tails from curling.
5. In a mixing bowl, combine the butter, achiote paste, and orange juice and zest. Place the prawns in the mixture and marinate in the refrigerator for 2 hours.
6. Make the potatoes: Preheat the oven to 325°F.

7 In a mixing bowl, stir together the cream, egg yolks, Parmesan, and pepper. Fold the potatoes into the mixture, then evenly fill 8 cavities of a muffin pan. Bake for 25 minutes, or until golden and tender. Remove from the oven.

8 Make the demi-glace: In a large saucepan over low heat, combine the demi-glace and mushrooms and slow simmer for 10 minutes. Transfer to a blender and blend until smooth. Strain the demi-glace mixture through a fine-mesh sieve into a gravy boat or similar serving dish and discard the solids.

9 To serve, preheat the oven to 400°F.

10 Place the prawns and their marinade in a baking dish and bake for 7–9 minutes, turning once during the cooking time. Remove from the oven.

11 Place the steaks on a baking sheet and reheat them until they reach the desired temperature.

12 While the steaks are reheating, loosen the potatoes from the muffin pan and transfer them to eight individual serving plates. Once the steaks are heated, remove them from the oven and place one on each serving plate. Pour some of the demi-glace over each steak and arrange the prawns resting against them. Garnish each plate with the serrano peppers, tomatoes, and sage and serve with the remaining demi-glace on the side.

Recipe by Michael Mata, executive chef, The St. Anthony

THE US GRANT
SAN DIEGO, CALIFORNIA, USA

THE US GRANT MANHATTAN

SERVES 1

2 oz High West double rye · 1 oz Dolin Rouge vermouth
3–6 drops Fee Brothers old fashion bitters
1 Luxardo maraschino cherry, for garnish

1. In a mixing glass filled with ice, combine the rye, vermouth, and bitters and stir.
2. Strain into a martini glass, garnish with the cherry, and serve.

Optional: To "age" this cocktail at home, fill a decanter of choice ⅘ full with the aforementioned recipe, top off with American oak chips, and set aside to steep for 100 days. Strain out and discard the chips. Transfer to a separate decanter.

"A modern interpretation of a classic cocktail, our Manhattan is a worthy homage to our namesake, President Ulysses S. Grant, and his fondness of whiskey."

JEFF JOSENHANS
director of banquets, restaurants, and bars

HIGH
WEST
WHISKEY
CENTENNIAL 100 DAY AGED MANHATTAN
MANHATTAN MADE WITH STRAIGHT RYE WHISKEY
BOTTLED BY HIGH WEST DISTILLERY
PARK CITY, UTAH AT DSP-UT-15001
001
Batch No.
001
Bottle No.
BOTTLED AT 46% ALCOHOL BY VOLUME

METRIC CONVERSIONS CHART

VOLUME

1 tsp = ⅓ tablespoon = ⅙ fl oz = 4 ml

1 Tbsp = 3 teaspoons = ½ fl oz = 15 ml

⅛ cup = 2 tablespoons = 1 fl oz = 30 ml

¼ cup = 4 tablespoons = 2 fl oz = 50 ml

⅓ cup = ¼ cup plus 4 tsp = 2¾ fl oz = 75 ml

½ cup = 8 tablespoons = 4 fl oz = 125 ml

¾ cup = 10 tablespoons = 6 fl oz = 175 ml

1 cup = ½ pint = 8 fl oz = 250 ml

1 pint = 16 fl oz = 2 cups = 500 ml

1 quart = 32 fl oz = 2 pints

1 liter = 34 fl oz = 1 quart plus ¼ cup

1 gallon = 128 fl oz = 4 quarts

TEMPERATURE

450°F = 230°C = 8 (hot)

425°F = 220°C = 7 (hot)

400°F = 200°C = 6 (moderately hot)

350°F = 180°C = 4 (moderate)

325°F = 165°C = 3 (moderate)

300°F = 150°C = 2 (slow)

250°F = 125°C = ½ (very slow)

225°F = 110°C = ¼ (very slow)

MASS

1 cup olive or vegetable oil, water, wine, vinegar = 236.6 ml (rounded above to 250ml)

½ oz = 14 grams

2 oz = 57 grams

3 oz = 85 grams

4 oz = 113 grams

5 oz = 142 grams

6 oz = 170 grams

8 oz = 227 grams

10 oz = 283 grams

12 oz = 340 grams

16 oz = 454 grams

RECIPE INDEX

STARTER

SALAD

SOUP

SIDE

MAIN

MAIN (CONT.)

DESSERT

DRINK

THE LUXURY COLLECTION HOTEL DIRECTORY

AFRICA

ETHIOPIA

SHERATON ADDIS

From the crystal clear pool with soft underwater music to the yearly Ethiopian art exhibition, the hotel is the perfect place to indulge and experience the culture of Addis Ababa.

Taitu Street, P.O. Box 6002
Addis Ababa
telephone 251 11 517 1717

theluxurycollection.com/addis

ASIA

CHINA

THE ASTOR HOTEL

Located in the heart of Tianjin, this architectural gem offers guests access to amenities such as a water-based treadmill and a hotel museum. It is also in walking distance of the Xiao Bai Lou, a pedestrian mall that guests can explore.

33 Taier Zhuang Road, Heping District
Tianjin 300040
telephone 86 22 5852 6888

theluxurycollection.com/astor

CHINA

THE AZURE QIANTANG

The mythic Qiantang River sets the scene at The Azure Qiantang, where the concierge recommends a private sculling boat trip to explore an ancient pilgrimage route and the largest tidal bore in the world.

39 East Wangjiang Road
Shangcheng District
Hangzhou, Zhejiang 310008
telephone 86 571 2823 7777

theluxurycollection.com/qiantang

CHINA

THE CASTLE HOTEL

Overlooking vibrant Xinghai Bay, The Castle Hotel boasts three sophisticated restaurants, a lounge, and a spa. Its grand ballrooms serve as settings for truly memorable occasions.

600 Binhai West Road
Shahekou District
Dalian, Liaoning 116023
telephone 86 411 8656 0000

theluxurycollection.com/castle

CHINA

THE GRAND MANSION

In the heart of Nanjing's cultural district, this iconic hotel unites the city's fabled past with destination dining and modern amenities.

300 Changjiang Road
Nanjing, Jiangsu 210005
telephone 86 25 8435 5888

theluxurycollection.com/grandmansion

CHINA

THE HONGTA HOTEL

Sweeping views of Shanghai, personalized butler service, and the award-winning Italian restaurant Danieli's make one's stay at The Hongta Hotel a first-class experience.

889 Dong Fang Road, Pudong District
Shanghai 200122
telephone 86 21 5050 4567

theluxurycollection.com/hongta

CHINA
MEIXI LAKE
Elegant accommodations and modern facilities blend into an urban oasis of serene lake views, captivating culture, and layered history.

1177 Huanhu Road
Changsha, Hunan 410006
telephone 86 731 8869 8888

theluxurycollection.com/meixilake

CHINA
THE ROYAL BEGONIA
Exceptional Spanish style, luxury settings, and personalized services combined with indigenous local attractions and culinary arts make this hotel a world-class destination. Our Begonia restaurant features authentic Southeast Asian cuisines complemented with typical Spanish signature dishes.

Haitang Beilu, Haitang Bay, Sanya
Haitang Bay, Hainan 572013
telephone 86 898 3885 9999

theluxurycollection.com/royalbegonia

CHINA
TWELVE AT HENGSHAN
Located on the beautiful tree-lined Hengshan Road, this modern, stylish newcomer is a stone's throw from the city's trendy shopping area, restaurants, parks, and museums.

12 Hengshan Road, Xuhui District
Shanghai 200031
telephone 86 21 3338 3888

luxurycollection.com/12hengshan

INDIA
ITC GARDENIA
Set in the commercial heart of Bengaluru, ITC Gardenia is a verdant sanctuary exuding natural sophistication and elegance. Combined with its ambience of nature embracing luxury, warm hospitality, and superlative facilities, ITC Gardenia lives the "Responsible Luxury" promise and is a tribute to the Garden City.

1 Residency Road, Bengaluru
Karnataka 560025
telephone 91 80 2211 9898

theluxurycollection.com/itcgardenia

INDIA
ITC GRAND BHARAT
The resort's 300 acres encompass elaborate culinary experiences, conference facilities, and recreation and wellness services. Envisioned as a supreme leisure getaway destination, the hotel is situated in an idyllic expanse, just outside Delhi, surrounded by the majestic Aravalli range and dotted with pristine lakes.

Gurgaon, New Delhi Capital Region
PO: Hasanpur, Dist: Mewat, Haryana 122105
telephone 91 1267 285 500

theluxurycollection.com/itcgrandbharat

INDIA
ITC GRAND CENTRAL
The palatial hotel evokes Mumbai's colonial grandeur with authentic décor and worldly amenities. ITC Grand Central represents the patchwork of Mumbai's cultures—its English charm, mercantile past, and modern present—effortlessly blending old and new Bombay.

Dr Babasaheb Ambedkar Road
Parel, Mumbai
Maharashtra 400012
telephone 91 22 2410 1010

theluxurycollection.com/itcgrandcentral

INDIA
ITC GRAND CHOLA
In its grandeur and majesty, this 600-room masterpiece is an inspired rendition of the vision of South India's great masters. With a perfect synergy of history, refined opulence, and unparalleled service, guests can enjoy an exceptional indigenous luxury experience.

63 Mount Road, Guindy, Chennai
Tamil Nadu 600032
telephone 91 44 2220 0000

theluxurycollection.com/itcgrandchola

INDIA
ITC KAKATIYA
Discover opulence in the heart of Hyderabad's commercial district, as authentic Kakatiya décor unites with singular views of Lake Hussain Sagar. This luxury hotel is a true homage to the legendary Kakatiya Dynasty.

6-3-1187 Begumpet, Hyderabad
Telangana 500016
telephone 91 40 2340 0132

theluxurycollection.com/itckakatiya

INDIA
ITC MARATHA
Elegance and history merge to reveal the city's rich culture. Saluting the legacy of the Grand Marathas, this hotel presents a range of cuisines, accommodations, and recreational options with the warmth of Indian hospitality for an unmistakably majestic experience.

Sahar Airport Road, Near International Airport
Mumbai, Maharashtra 400099
telephone 91 22 2830 3030

theluxurycollection.com/itcmaratha

INDIA
ITC MAURYA
Situated in the diplomatic enclave of New Delhi, with more than 400 luxurious rooms and suites, in addition to world-renowned cuisine and a deep understanding of the needs of the global traveler, this hotel is the preferred accommodation for heads of state, royalty, and business leaders.

Diplomatic Enclave
New Delhi 110021
telephone 91 11 2611 2233

theluxurycollection.com/itcmaurya

INDIA
ITC MUGHAL
Sprawled over 35 acres of lush gardens and water features near the magnificent Taj Mahal, this hotel is a tribute to the Mughal era. ITC Mughal boasts the country's largest and most luxurious spa, Kaya Kalp–the Royal Spa, along with a range of fine-dining options.

Taj Ganj, Agra
Uttar Pradesh 282001
telephone 91 562 402 1700

theluxurycollection.com/itcmughal

INDIA
ITC RAJPUTANA
Centrally located, ITC Rajputana is the perfect blend of Rajasthani architecture and Rajput hospitality. The *haveli*-inspired architecture and regal design echo the city's history, while the balconies from the guest rooms face an intricate network of internal courtyards.

Palace Road, Jaipur
Rajasthan 302006
telephone 91 141 510 0100

theluxurycollection.com/itcrajputana

INDIA
ITC SONAR
Celebrating the Golden Era of Bengal, ITC Sonar is a verdant oasis just minutes from the heart of Kolkata. Garden houses, large green spaces, and water features reminiscent of the Baghbaris create a captivating setting, while a well-appointed spa provides modern-day comforts in the City of Joy.

JBS Haldane Avenue, Kolkata
West Bengal 700046
telephone 91 33 2345 4545

theluxurycollection.com/itcsonar

INDIA
ITC WINDSOR
ITC Windsor's elegant colonnades, fluted pillars, Georgian windows, and magnificent chandeliers create a stirring ambience of old-world leisure. Experience the glory of the days of the Raj, minutes from downtown Bengaluru, where the colonial past meets modern luxury.

Windsor Square, 25, Golf Course Road
Bangaluru, Karnataka 560052
telephone 91 80 2226 9898

theluxurycollection.com/itcwindsor

INDONESIA
KERATON AT THE PLAZA
This beautiful hotel celebrates the richness of Indonesian culture and local Javanese traditions through its art gallery and cuisine.

Jl. MH. Thamrin Kav. 15
Jakarta 10350
telephone 62 21 5068 0000

theluxurycollection.com/keraton

INDONESIA
THE LAGUNA
Nestled on Bali's finest white-sand beach overlooking the majestic Indian Ocean and infinite swimmable lagoons, The Laguna is situated perfectly in the enchanting Nusa Dua enclave.

Kawasan Pariwisata Nusa Dua Lot N2
Nusa Dua, Bali 80363
telephone 62 361 771327

theluxurycollection.com/bali

JAPAN
THE PRINCE GALLERY TOKYO KIOICHO
Near businesses and landmarks in Tokyo's most dignified neighborhood, guests are welcomed in innovative interiors and upscale guest rooms.

1-2 Kioi-cho Chiyoda-ku, Tokyo
telephone 81 3 3234 1111

theluxurycollection.com/princegallery

JAPAN
SUIRAN
This hotel offers authentic Japanese experiences within a historic Kyoto community—a peaceful riverfront haven steps from the Tenryu-ji, World Heritage Site.

Saga-Tenryuji, Ukyo-Ku
12 Susukinobaba-Cho
Kyoto
telephone 81 75 872 0101

theluxurycollection.com/suiran

MALAYSIA
THE ANDAMAN
Stunning sunsets, crystal blue waters, rainforest trails, and coral reef walks are just some of the extraordinary experiences this hotel offers guests.

Jalan Teluk Datai
Langkawi, 07000
telephone 60 4 959 1088

theluxurycollection.com/andaman

THAILAND
THE NAKA ISLAND
With endless views of Phang Nga Bay and the Phuket landscape, this five-star island retreat is private, romantic, and idyllic.

32 Moo 5, Tambol Paklok
Amphur Thalang, Naka Yai Island
Phuket 83110
telephone 66 76 371 400

theluxurycollection.com/nakaisland

THAILAND
SHERATON GRANDE SUKHUMVIT
This hotel is home to Basil, one of the finest Thai restaurants in Bangkok, where chef Kesinee Wanta crafts creative dishes with the exquisite flavors from every culinary region of Thailand.

250 Sukhumvit Road
Bangkok 10110
telephone 66 2 649 8888

theluxurycollection.com/grandesukhumvit

THAILAND

VANA BELLE

Poised overlooking the breathtaking Gulf of Siam, Vana Belle offers an enchanting getaway and memorable experiences in one of Thailand's most beautiful locations.

9/99 Moo 3, Chaweng Noi Beach, Surat Thani
Koh Samui 84320
telephone 66 77 915 555

theluxurycollection.com/vanabellesamui

EUROPE

AUSTRIA

HOTEL BRISTOL

Located near the Vienna State Opera in the heart of the city, this luxury hotel provides an oasis from the bustle of a busy metropolis. The concierge recommends visiting the elegant Winter Palace of Prince Eugene of Savoy, right in the city center.

Kaerntner Ring 1
Vienna 1010
telephone 43 1 515 160

theluxurycollection.com/bristol

AUSTRIA

HOTEL GOLDENER HIRSCH

Sip the signature Susanne cocktail, eat the famous Rigo Jancsi dessert, and live in luxury while attending nearby summer festivals in Salzburg.

Getreidegasse 37
Salzburg 5020
telephone 43 6 628 0840

theluxurycollection.com/goldenerhirsch

AUSTRIA

HOTEL IMPERIAL

Experience the essence of Vienna at this elegant and beautiful hotel and delight in the Viennese coffee tradition by enjoying a cup of Imperial coffee and a slice of the renowned torte.

Kaerntner Ring 16
Vienna, 1015
telephone 43 1 501 100

theluxurycollection.com/imperial

AUSTRIA

SCHLOSS FUSCHL

Enjoy a valuable collection of Old Masters, a lush golf course, and fresh fish from the castle fishery at this hotel.

Schloss Strasse 19
Hof bei Salzburg 5322
telephone 43 6 229 22530

theluxurycollection.com/schlossfuschl

BULGARIA

SOFIA HOTEL BALKAN

Located in downtown Sofia, this luxury hotel offers an exceptional experience of Bulgaria's finest culture and service.

5 Sveta Nedelya Square
Sofia 1000
telephone 359 2 981 6541

theluxurycollection.com/sofia

CZECH REPUBLIC

AUGUSTINE

Located in a thirteenth-century Augustinian monastery, the hotel boasts impeccable service and design inspired by early-twentieth-century Czech cubism.

Letenská 12/33
Prague 1 110 00
telephone 420 2 6611 2233

theluxurycollection.com/augustine

FRANCE

PRINCE DE GALLES

Just steps away from the Champs-Élysées, this Art Deco hotel, a mosaic of discrete Parisian elegance, is located in the heart of the city and offers exceptional hospitality and superb cuisine by culinary talent Stéphanie Le Quellec.

33 Avenue George V
Paris 75008
telephone 33 1 53 237777

theluxurycollection.com/princedegalles

GERMANY

HOTEL ELEPHANT

Fine dining, cooking lessons with Michelin-starred chef Marcello Fabbri, and guided cultural tours are all offered at this unique hotel.

Markt 19
Weimar 99423
telephone 49 3643 8020

theluxurycollection.com/elephant

GERMANY

HOTEL FUERSTENHOF

Relax in the AquaMarin spa, the landscaped pool, the Finnish sauna, or the Roman steam bath and restore harmony to your body at this luxury hotel.

Troendlinring 8
Leipzig 04105
telephone 49 341 1400

theluxurycollection.com/fuerstenhof

GREECE

BLUE PALACE

Discover beauty in this hotel's emblematic views, tranquility at its Elounda Spa on the beach, and fun at the nearby Crete Golf Club.

P.O. Box 38
Elounda, Crete 72053
telephone 30 284 106 5500

theluxurycollection.com/bluepalace

GREECE

HOTEL GRANDE BRETAGNE

With unsurpassed views of the Acropolis and Parthenon, Constitution Square, and Lycabettus Hill, this hotel offers unrivaled access to Athens's mythical history.

Vas Georgiou A' Street 1
Athens 10564
telephone 30 210 333 0000

theluxurycollection.com/grandebretagne

GREECE

KING GEORGE

Just two kilometers from the Acropolis, this hotel has welcomed many celebrities and hosted many events in its 350-square-meter room under the illuminated sky.

Vas Georgiou A' Street 3
Athens 10564
telephone 30 210 322 2210

theluxurycollection.com/kinggeorge

GREECE

MYSTIQUE

Guests can visit the Secret Wine Cave, take in the beauty of the surrounding views, and restore at the spa while visiting this luxury resort.

Oia
Santorini Island
Santorini, South Aegean 84702
telephone 30 228 607 1114

theluxurycollection.com/mystique

GREECE

THE ROMANOS

Guests can indulge in one of Anazoe Spa's signature treatments, experience tours from Navarino Outdoors, and scuba dive with Navarino Sea—all experiences that can be arranged by the concierge.

Navarino Dunes, Messinia
Costa Navarino 24001
telephone 30 272 309 6000

theluxurycollection.com/theromanos

GREECE

SANTA MARINA

A paradise within a paradise, this hotel is a tranquil oasis where one can indulge in spa treatments and fine dining surrounded by the natural beauty of Mykonos.

Ornos Bay
Mykonos, South Aegean 84600
telephone 30 228 902 3220

theluxurycollection.com/santamarina

GREECE

VEDEMA

Surrounded by historical sites, beautiful beaches, and hot springs, this luxury resort has plenty to explore.

Megalohori
Santorini, South Aegean 84700
telephone 30 228 608 1796

theluxurycollection.com/vedema

ITALY

CRISTALLO

Complete relaxation, elegant cuisine, and natural beauty await guests of this resort's refined facilities and fin de siècle atmosphere.

Via Rinaldo Menardi 42
Cortina d'Ampezzo 32043
telephone 39 043 688 1111

theluxurycollection.com/cristallo

ITALY

EXCELSIOR HOTEL GALLIA

Located at the heart of fashion capital Milan, Excelsior Hotel Gallia provides the ideal setting for sophistication. The concierge suggests an evening at the world-renowned La Scala Opera House.

Piazza Duca D'Aosta 9
Milan 20124
telephone 39 02 67851

theluxurycollection.com/excelsiorgallia

ITALY

FALISIA

Indulge in delectable multicultural cuisine and indelible experiences in and along the Gulf of Trieste.

Località Sistiana 231/M
Portopiccolo 34011
telephone 39 040 997 4444

theluxurycollection.com/falisia

ITALY

THE GRITTI PALACE

Occupying a prestigious setting on the Grand Canal, The Gritti Palace recently reopened after a meticulous restoration. A leisurely short stroll from Piazza San Marco, the imposing palazzo awards rare views of Santa Maria della Salute.

Campo Santa Maria del Giglio
Venice 30124
telephone 39 0417 94611

theluxurycollection.com/grittipalace

ITALY

HOTEL CALA DI VOLPE

Horseback riding, tennis, and golf are just some of the fun outdoor activities to enjoy at this hotel.

Costa Smeralda
Porto Cervo 07020
telephone 39 0789 976111

theluxurycollection.com/caladivolpe

ITALY

HOTEL DANIELI

Located within walking distance of Saint Mark's Square, this legendary hotel allows visitors to shop, dine, and experience Venice to the fullest.

Castello 4196
Venice 30122
telephone 39 041 522 6480

theluxurycollection.com/danieli

ITALY

HOTEL PITRIZZA

Experience local traditions and cuisine firsthand with the hotel's full immersion opportunities, including local artisan demonstrations.

Costa Smeralda
Porto Cervo 07020
telephone 39 0789 930111

theluxurycollection.com/hotelpitrizza

ITALY

HOTEL ROMAZZINO

Enjoy local food and activities such as horseback riding and sailing at this beautiful resort.

Costa Smeralda
Porto Cervo 07020
telephone 39 0789 977111

theluxurycollection.com/romazzino

THE NETHERLANDS

HOTEL DES INDES

This luxury hotel is located in the heart of The Hague and is an ideal starting point for exploring local attractions such as the Royal Picture Gallery Mauritshuis and the antique market.

Lange Voorhout 54-56
The Hague 2514 EG
telephone 31 70 361 2345

theluxurycollection.com/desindes

POLAND

HOTEL BRISTOL

This hotel lies right on the Royal Route, a road that leads through the historic district of the city and is dotted with examples of stunning architecture from the sixteenth century to the present day.

Krakowskie Przedmiescie 42/44
Warsaw 00-325
telephone 48 22 551 1000

theluxurycollection.com/bristolwarsaw

PORTUGAL

CONVENTO DO ESPINHEIRO

Enjoy wine-tasting sessions, bread-baking classes, Alentejo folk-singing performances, and Gregorian chants at this luxury resort.

Convento do Espinheiro
Évora 7000
telephone 351 266 788200

theluxurycollection.com/convento

PORTUGAL

PINE CLIFFS

Enjoy breathtaking views of the surroundings, warm weather year-round, and the beautiful golf course, including its famed and most challenging golf hole, Devil's Parlour, at this luxury hotel.

Praia de Falesia, Apartado P.O. Box 644
Algarve 8200
telephone 351 289 500100

theluxurycollection.com/algarve

RUSSIA

HOTEL NATIONAL

Exploring Moscow was never easier, as this hotel offers spectacular views of the Kremlin and Red Square, while being only steps away from attractions such as the Bolshoi Theatre.

15/1 Mokhovaya Street
Moscow 125009
telephone 7 495 258 7000

theluxurycollection.com/national

SERBIA

METROPOL PALACE

This hotel has always been the heart of Belgrade's social life and is an indelible landmark in the city skyline, overlooking Tasmajdan Park.

Bulevar Kralja Aleksandra 69
Belgrade 11000
telephone 381 11 333 3100

theluxurycollection.com/metropolpalace

SLOVAKIA

GRAND HOTEL RIVER PARK

The Slovakian capital's leading hotel is distinguished by its accessibility, sleek décor, spacious accommodations, and expansive spa.

Dvorakovo Nabrezie 6
Bratislava 81102
telephone 421 2 32238 222

theluxurycollection.com/grandhotelriverpark

SPAIN

CASTILLO HOTEL SON VIDA

A first-class beauty spa, breathtaking golf courses, and a Kids' Club equipped with a separate pool area and playground are all offered at this hotel.

C/Raixa 2, Urbanizacion Son Vida
Mallorca 07013
telephone 34 971 493493

theluxurycollection.com/castillo

SPAIN

HOTEL ALFONSO XIII

This hotel is one of the most monumental landmarks in Seville, embodying the city's layered history, architecture, and authentic cuisine in a luxurious atmosphere.

San Fernando 2
Seville 41004
telephone 34 95 491 7000

theluxurycollection.com/hotelalfonso

SPAIN

HOTEL MARIA CRISTINA

Indulge in a mouthwatering local culinary experience when visiting this charming hotel, near the Michelin-starred restaurants of San Sebastián.

Paseo Republica Argentina 4
San Sebastián 20004
telephone 34 943 437600

theluxurycollection.com/mariacristina

SPAIN

HOTEL MARQUÉS DE RISCAL

Frank Gehry's design houses a collection of wines that any wine lover will enjoy. The hotel offers guided cultural tours to truly take in the surrounding area.

Calle Torrea 1
Elciego 01340
telephone 34 945 180880

theluxurycollection.com/marquesderiscal

SWITZERLAND

HOTEL PRESIDENT WILSON

Located minutes away from Geneva's lakefront, this luxury hotel allows one to explore such local attractions as the Jet d'Eau, Flower Clock, and St. Peter's Cathedral.

47, Quai Wilson
Geneva 1211
telephone 41 22 906 6666

theluxurycollection.com/presidentwilson

TURKEY

CARESSE

Truly indulgent ESPA treatments, a picnic on a private yacht, breathtaking views from relaxing accommodations—all are possible here.

Adnan Menderes caddesi No. 89
Asarlik Mevkii PK 225
Bodrum 48400

telephone 90 252 311 3636

theluxurycollection.com/caresse

TURKEY

LUGAL

Immerse yourself in local culture, as original paintings by local artists are found throughout this luxury hotel.

Noktali Sokak No. 1, 'Kavaklidere
Ankara 06700
telephone 90 312 457 6050

theluxurycollection.com/lugal

UNITED KINGDOM

THE PARK TOWER KNIGHTSBRIDGE

While at this hotel, guests can visit the vibrant Serpentine Gallery, and dine at One-O-One, which is under the auspices of acclaimed chef Pascal Proyart and is recognized as the city's best fish restaurant by critics and locals alike.

101 Knightsbridge
London, Great Britain SW1X 7RN
telephone 44 207 235 8050

theluxurycollection.com/parktowerlondon

UNITED KINGDOM

TRUMP TURNBERRY

From world-class golfing facilities, including the nine-hole Arran course, to quad biking and horseback riding, to private tours of the magnificent surrounding areas, which can be arranged by the concierge, this luxury hotel is an outdoorsman's sanctuary.

Turnberry Ayrshire KA26 9LT
Scotland
telephone 44 165 533 1000

theluxurycollection.com/trumpturnberry

UNITED KINGDOM

THE WELLESLEY KNIGHTSBRIDGE

Boutique and grand elements exist harmoniously in this Knightsbridge hotel near fabled parks, renowned shopping, and historic landmarks.

London, Great Britain SW1X 7LY
telephone 44 20 7235 3535

theluxurycollection.com/wellesleyknightsbridge

UNITED KINGDOM

THE WESTBURY

Thoughtfully redesigned accommodations and elegant facilities distinguish this hotel in Mayfair, near renowned fashion destinations.

37 Conduit Street
London, Great Britain W1S 2YF
telephone 44 207 629 7755

theluxurycollection.com/westbury

LATIN AMERICA

ARGENTINA

PARK TOWER

Unparalleled service, an in-hotel shopping arcade, and a heart-of-the-city location set this luxury hotel apart.

Avenida Leandro N. Alem 1193
Buenos Aires 1001
telephone 54 11 4318 9100

theluxurycollection.com/parktower

CHILE

SAN CRISTOBAL TOWER

A bicycle tour of the bohemian Bellavista neighborhood, picnics at the nearby Concha y Toro Vineyard, and skiing on the best slopes in South America are all offered at this luxury hotel.

Josefina Edwards de Ferrari 0100
Santiago
telephone 56 2 2707 1000

theluxurycollection.com/sancristobaltower

MEXICO
HACIENDA PUERTA CAMPECHE

This hotel is a collection of restored seventeenth-century historical houses, allowing one to enjoy the beauty of a Mexican hacienda with excellent personal service.

Calle 59, No. 71 por 16 & 18
Campeche, Campeche 24000
telephone 52 981 816 7508

theluxurycollection.com/puertacampeche

MEXICO
HACIENDA SAN JOSE

An authentic Mayan experience can be had in the Mayan Villas, while luxury can be found through massages in the privacy of the spa area.

KM 30 Carretera Tixkokob-Tekanto
Tixkokob, Yucatán 97470
telephone 52 999 924 1333

theluxurycollection.com/sanjose

MEXICO
HACIENDA SANTA ROSA

Bird watching, Mayan lessons, cocktail demonstrations, and tours of the botanical garden are all offered at this luxury hotel.

KM 129 Carretera Merida Campeche
Santa Rosa, Yucatán 97800
telephone 52 999 923 1923

theluxurycollection.com/santarosa

MEXICO
HACIENDA TEMOZON

Explore the unique Hol Be Spa, where one can experience individual spa treatments in a beautifully preserved cavern.

KM 182 Carretera Merida-Uxmal
Temozon Sur, Yucatán 97825
telephone 52 999 923 8089

theluxurycollection.com/temozon

MEXICO
HACIENDA UAYAMON

Bulbous pegs set into stone walls can be found throughout this hotel, allowing guests to hang woven cotton hammocks and sleep in the Mayan style.

KM 20 Carretera Uayamon-China-Edzná
Uayamon, Campeche
telephone 52 981 813 0530

theluxurycollection.com/uayamon

MEXICO
LAS ALCOBAS

Refined hospitality and unforgettable wellbeing and culinary experiences await in this hotel's artistic fusion of modernity, elegance, and comfort.

Ave. Presidente Masaryk 390
Mexico City, Federal District 11560
telephone 52 55 3300 3900

theluxurycollection.com/
lasalcobasmexicocity

PERU
PALACIO DEL INKA

Located in the historic center of Cusco, this hotel dates back almost five centuries and offers easy access to museums, markets, and restaurants. Its property also boasts a relaxing therapy pool.

Plazoleta Santo Domingo 259
Cusco
telephone 51 84 231 961

theluxurycollection.com/palaciodelinka

PERU
HOTEL PARACAS

A bottle of local pisco, wind-surfing lessons, and private-jet flights over the Nazca Lines are all offered at this luxury hotel. The concierge suggests traveling back in time with a visit to the intriguing archaeological site Tambo Colorado.

Av. Paracas S/N
Paracas
telephone 51 56 581 333

theluxurycollection.com/hotelparacas

PERU
TAMBO DEL INKA

Enjoy views of the Vilcanota River while swimming in the hotel pool. Take a guided trip to the Valle Sagrado and escape to Machu Picchu from the hotel's private train station.

Avenida Ferrocarril S/N
Sacred Valley, Urubamba
telephone 51 84 581 777

theluxurycollection.com/tambodelinka

MIDDLE EAST

KUWAIT
SHERATON KUWAIT

Situated in the middle of Kuwait's commercial center, the hotel boasts a health club that offers a variety of revitalizing, relaxing, and pampering treatments.

Safat 13060 / Fahd Al-Salem Street
P.O. Box 5902 Safat
Kuwait City 13060
telephone 965 2242 2055

theluxurycollection.com/kuwait

LEBANON
GRAND HILLS

Lush greenery and pine forests carpet the locale of Grand Hills, and the nearby Beirut coast offers amazing Mediterranean views. For the more adventurous, the concierge suggests traveling up the coast to Byblos, the world's oldest continually inhabited city.

Charkieh Main Road
Broumana 1204
telephone 961 4 868 888

theluxurycollection.com/grandhills

U.A.E.
AJMAN SARAY

Situated along the Arabian Gulf, just minutes from Dubai, this resort overlooks endless expanses of pristine sand and shimmering sea.

Sheikh Humaid Bin Rashid Al Nuaimi Street
Ajman 8833
telephone 971 6 714 2222

theluxurycollection.com/ajmansaray

U.A.E.
AL MAHA

Arabian wildlife—with Arabian oryx and gazelles as the star attractions—can be seen from the temperature-controlled infinity pools or sundeck areas of all villas.

Dubai–Al Ain Road
Dubai
telephone 971 4 832 9900

theluxurycollection.com/almaha

U.A.E.
GROSVENOR HOUSE

This lifestyle destination, located in the cosmopolitan area of Dubai Marina, offers access to fantastic restaurants, including the hotel's world-famous Buddha Bar.

Al Sofouh Road
P.O. Box 118500
Dubai
telephone 971 4 399 8888

theluxurycollection.com/grosvenorhouse

NORTH AMERICA

UNITED STATES
THE BALLANTYNE

Located on a championship PGA golf course, this Southern beauty features signature cocktails, luxurious lodging, and spa treatments.

10000 Ballantyne Commons Parkway
Charlotte, North Carolina 28277
telephone 1 704 248 4000

theluxurycollection.com/ballantyne